The Savage My Kinsman

By Elisabeth Elliot

Photographs By

Elisabeth Elliot
Cornell Capa

Servant Books • Ann Arbor, Michigan

Originally published in 1961, this revised editon is
published in 1981 by Servant Books
                    P.O. Box 8617
                    Ann Arbor, Michigan 48107

Cover illustration by Jim Lamb
Book design by John B. Leidy

Photographs by Cornell Capa are used with his permission.
In addition, special acknowledgment is due to the following
persons for the photographs reproduced on the pages indicated: Nate Saint (opposite foreword, p. 3, and p. 8) and
Major Malcolm Nurnberg (top p. 7).

Printed in the United States of America
ISBN 0-89283-099-9

Contents

Acknowledgments

Some of the pictures in this book were taken by Cornell Capa. The rest of them, with a few exceptions, were taken because of him. It was he who first encouraged me to get a camera, and then gave me some lessons in how to use it. Whatever is acceptable in my pictures is due mostly to what I absorbed of those lessons, and partly to what is commonly called luck. While I lived with the Aucas I tried to make a pictorial record, and I sent my film to Cornell. He decided that there were enough pictures to make up the book that my publishers had requested me to prepare before I entered Auca territory. He did all of the editing and initial layout of the pictures for the original edition, and he read the text and offered suggestions for revision. He has helped me in more ways than I can enumerate, and I am very grateful.

E. E.

Note on the Spelling of
Auca Words and Names

At the time that this book was first published, the Auca language had not been "reduced to writing." This does not mean that it had never been written. Rachel Saint and I recorded a large amount of material, using phonetic characters. Any sound produced by the human voice may be so recorded. But to reduce a language to writing means to determine, by scientific analysis, which of these characters are *necessary* to that language. When all of the superfluous letters have been eliminated, we have what is called a phonemic alphabet. We could not be sure that the orthography we were using for the Auca language was entirely phonemic, hence there may be discrepancies between spellings—for example, we have at least two different "a's" in the Auca language. One is roughly equivalent to that in "cat," the other to that in "father." In some cases the former has been spelled "ae," the latter simply "a." There are nasalized vowels, lengthened vowels, and other examples of letters which cannot be easily recorded in our English alphabet, but for simplicity we did not try to be completely consistent.

Foreword

I N THE WINTER of 1956 I was asked by *Life* magazine to fly down to Ecuador to find out what had happened to five American missionaries who had been reported missing in the jungle.

Many hard-to-believe things have happened since then and this book is the latest chapter of the most remarkable missionary story of the century.

For those who possibly missed the first installment of the story as it was detailed in *Life* magazine and in Elisabeth Elliot's book *Through Gates of Splendor*, it is important to retell the beginnings.

Five missionaries—Pete Fleming, Roger Youderian, Ed McCully, Nate Saint, and Betty's husband, Jim Elliot—all young, all married, all, except one, fathers—planned to make contact with a mysterious, almost legendary Indian tribe that dwells in the depths of the Amazon jungle. Only one fact was known with certainty about the Aucas: they killed every outsider who came near them. For months, and with great attention to details, the young men planned their "Operation Auca," until finally they felt the time was right for the first important attempt to meet the Aucas.

On January 3, l956, in a plane piloted by Nate Saint, the young Americans established a beachhead in Auca territory on the Curaray River—a narrow strip of sand which they named "Palm Beach." There, they constructed a tree-house, improvised a two-way radio contact with Nate's wife, Marj, in Shell Mera, and settled down on the beach in the hope of meeting members of the tribe.

During the first day on the beach Nate flew over the nearby settlement of thatched huts which the missionaries named "Terminal City," trying by gestures and shouting over a loudspeaker to persuade the Indians to visit Palm Beach.

For three days the missionaries waited patiently by the river, fishing and making notes in their diaries. Suddenly, on the morning of January 6, from directly across the river, they heard the boom of a strong masculine voice, and immediately thereafter an Auca man and two women stepped out into the open. The five men shouted *"Puinani!"* ("Welcome!"), then Jim Elliot waded across the shallow twenty yards that separated them. He took the Indians by the hand and led them back to his side.

The Auca man was a young fellow, one of the women perhaps thirty or so, and the other a girl about sixteen. Except for a string or two they were completely naked. The missionaries nicknamed the man "George" and the young girl "Delilah."

The three Aucas spent the day on Palm Beach. Then, as suddenly as they had come, they walked away into the jungle. The missionaries settled down to wait for their return, hoping that more of the tribe would follow the first friendly encounter.

They came. In the late afternoon of January 8 they speared the missionaries and left them to die.

Meanwhile, Marj Saint and the other wives waited in vain for

Jim Elliot was delighted that the three Aucas—an older woman, a young one nicknamed "Delilah," and a man called "George"—came out of the jungle to meet the five missionaries.

the radio contact Nate had promised for that same afternoon. The next day, when the ominous silence from Palm Beach remained unbroken, fears grew that something had gone wrong. Another missionary pilot, Johnny Keenan, volunteered to fly over the beach. Keeping his plane low, he spotted the wing of Nate's Piper lying on the sand, stripped of its yellow sheathing. No life was visible around it. A rescue party was formed at once, made up of Ecuadorian soldiers, American missionaries, and Quichua Indians, under the leadership of Frank Drown, another missionary.

Traveling through the jungle, following the winding Curaray, on foot and in canoes, they reached Palm Beach in three days. After searching the area, they found the spear-riddled bodies of the five men on the beach and floating in the water.

The Air Force Rescue Service's helicopter landed and I jumped out just as the rescue party was taking the last body to a common grave. The atmosphere was fantastic: nervous hands fingered triggers and eyes were trained on the oppressive wall of jungle. I did not have to ask why. A storm came on with tropical suddenness, rain fell in buckets, dim figures moved through an eerie light. Grim and weary missionaries looked for the last time at their friends, whose bodies they could no longer identify. One of them said, "It's better this way. I feel less miserable."

There followed our homeward trek through Auca territory. The canoes, overloaded, leaked at the slightest movement and I sat, like a protective mother hen, shielding my cameras from the water. Major Malcolm Nurnberg, an American Air Force attaché from Quito, led the party—with his carbine poised at all times—out of the danger area.

At the missionary base of Shell Mera, five women were waiting for our return. Through radio communication, they knew that all were lost, but they wanted to be told, in minute detail, everything that had happened. Dr. Art Johnston, who was in the rescue party, spared them nothing as he faced them in the kitchen of Nate

The rescue party, led by Major Nurnberg, travels warily back upriver.

Saint's home. Their faces were drawn and gaunt, but there were no complaints, no self-pity.

I flew back to New York, carrying with me the pictures of Operation Auca taken by Nate Saint. Among them was the last strip of film developed out of his camera that had been found in the river. It showed the three Aucas of this hitherto unphotographed tribe. The men's diaries gave many details of the missionary contact with them, but the hopes of ever finding out exactly what had occurred on the beach and why the seemingly friendly contact had turned into massacre were slim indeed. The answer lay buried deep in the jungle with the unreachable Aucas.

For me, at least, the story seemed to have come to an end. The widows believed that their husbands' death was not the meaningless tragedy it appeared to many. No thoughts of revenge crossed their minds; on the contrary, they felt with an increased sense of urgency the need to bring their message of love and redemption to the Aucas. During the following year I learned of the quiet determination with which the widows continued their work in the missionary field right in Ecuador. Marj Saint and Marilou McCully, with three children each, moved to Quito to work in missionary headquarters; Betty Elliot and Barbara Youderian stayed in the jungle with their small families, working among the Quichua and Jivaro Indians. I decided to visit them again and try to understand the urge that lay behind their extraordinary dedication. The peace of soul, the mental and physical security shown by all those I had visited, defied my comprehension. They never stopped praying and hoping that one day the Aucas might make their first hesitant steps to the outside world.

I visited Betty at the Quichua mission station of Shandia. It was strange to see this gaunt, tall, blonde American woman walk through the jungle, often shoeless because it was easier that way, but with a wary eye for poisonous snakes. With her, also barefoot, went her daughter, Valerie, a tiny ethereal creature who

Dr. Johnston described in detail how they found the bodies of the men. The truth was inescapable – all five were dead.

seemed to walk not on the earth but slightly above it. Betty taught at the school that Jim and Pete Fleming had re-established, did medical work, and continued translating parts of the Bible into the Quichua tongue. Betty was firm on everything that involved her faith, Valerie, and herself: "Where I go Valerie goes. I believe the Lord expects me to be as careful as possible about Valerie's health in our home, but when I accept the hospitality from the Indians I trust the Lord to take care of the results. I feel it is more important for me and Valerie to share the Indian life, than to cut ourselves off from them in order to preserve our health." I wondered how Betty could reconcile Jim's death at the hands of the Aucas and the Lord's apparent failure to protect him from them. Her answer came back without hesitation: "I prayed for the protection of Jim, that is, physical protection. The answer the Lord gave transcended what I had in mind. He gave protection from disobedience and through Jim's death accomplished results the magnitude of which only Eternity can show." I left Shandia a bit shaken and kept on hearing Betty's parting words: "It gives me a much more personal desire to reach them. The fact that Jesus Christ died for all makes me interested in the salvation of all, but the fact that Jim loved and died for the Aucas intensifies my love for them."

Another year passed by. Then the news came that two Auca women had emerged from the jungle, that Betty had met them and taken them into her home in Shandia. I heard, too, that one of the Aucas was the older woman who had been among the last to see Jim and his fellow missionaries alive on Palm Beach.

I felt impelled to go back to Ecuador and see Betty with her strange guests. It was during this visit, as I watched Betty with her new friends, that I gained a deeper insight into the character of this remarkable American woman.

The rest of her story is in this book. She did go to meet the tribe. Betty and Valerie, together with Nate Saint's sister, Rachel, lived with the Aucas for almost a year. Then Betty

The damaged film found in Nate Saint's camera, submerged in the Curaray after his death.

returned with her notes and her photographs.

I would like to say a few words about the photographs. Betty was no photographer and her interest lay in her missionary and language work. She saw me work with the camera during my three visits in the jungle and we had many chances to talk about our individual "missions." I was able to convince her of the value of the camera as an irreplaceable means of communication and expression. I explained the camera as a simple mechanical instrument, easy to operate: all she had to do was to use it as an extension of her eyes, to photograph subjects she cared about: her daughter and her Indians.

The results are in this book for you to see.

CORNELL CAPA

Introduction

WHEN THEY FIRST heard that savage Indians known as Aucas had killed five American missionaries in the jungles of South America in 1956, many people asked, "Are there still such savages living today?" The obvious yes to that question gave rise to further questions. Why did they do it? Who are they? How do they live? What makes them savage?

Then when three of us went to live in the tribe with these people, we were asked, "How do they respond toward you? How do you feel toward them? What are you trying to do?"

I am not sure I can fully answer these questions. I have lived with the Aucas less than a year and must limit myself mostly to description rather than explanation of the Auca people. I know far too little of their language even to understand much of what they say, let alone what they think. I can barely hold up my end of a conversation dealing with the simplest everyday matters. I know next to nothing of tribal lore, superstitions, religion, thought patterns, and beliefs.

My speculations concerning the Aucas' attitudes toward outsiders, the reasons for their former behavior, their nature and character proved to be quite wrong. Ideas I had had about how to approach them were turned upside down, and my perspective on my own society was changed. I felt in many ways that I knew less, after living with the Aucas, than I had known when I went in. My hammock by the fire became an ivory tower. I was isolated from my own people by distance, from the Aucas by being a foreigner. Unable to communicate, I was forced to reflect.

And I did take some pictures. I made notes on what I saw. It is my hope that these will convey some idea of who the Aucas are, how they live, how we lived with them, and some of the problems we faced. Perhaps the contemplation of this society may give a new perspective on our own and help us to know what it is that really matters.

The word "missionary" may call to mind preaching, teaching, church-building (and even this often means merely a physical plant, rather than a spiritual building), medical work, baptizing, catechizing, social improvement—almost any form of philanthropy. I found myself quite unable to undertake any one of these activities. A strange position for one who was called a missionary. I began to search my Guidebook to learn whether my definition had been an accurate one. The word "missionary" does not occur in the Bible. But the word "witness" does. I found many passages indicating that I was supposed to be a witness. One in particular arrested me. It stated that to be a witness to God is, above all, to know, believe, and understand *Him*.[1] All that He asks us to do is but means to this end. He will go to any lengths to teach us, and His manipulation of the movements of men— Aucas, missionaries, whomever—is never accidental. Those movements may be *incidental* to the one thing toward which He goads us: the recognition of Christ.

---

[1] Isaiah 43:10.

1

"I Must Tread Alone"

WHEN ON JANUARY 16, 1956, the party of missionary volunteers, Quichua Indians, Ecuadorian soldiers, and American airmen who had gone to search for the five missing men returned to tell us that they were all dead, there was little sense of drama for me. The history of missions had repeated itself. I could see that, for I had read stories of missionaries, from the Benedictine monks who crossed the Alps into Germany and were murdered by savage tribesmen, to nineteenth-century Englishmen who went to the South Sea Islands and were clubbed to death. The crusading spirit, the thrill of reaching an unreached tribe, the passion for souls which is supposed to motivate some—all these faded out completely. I knew that if life was to go on, it must go on meaningfully. I was forced back to the real reasons for missionary work—indeed, the real reasons for living at all. My husband Jim and the four men who had gone into Auca territory had one reason: they believed it was what God wanted them to do. They took quite literally the words "The world passeth away and the lust thereof, but he that doeth the will of God abideth forever." It is only in obeying God that we may know Him. Obedience, if it is a good reason for dying, is just as good a reason for living. I knew that there was no other answer for me. The "whys" that screamed themselves at me day and night could not be silenced, but I could live with them if I simply went on and did the next thing.

Jim and I had been working among the Quichua Indians in a place called Shandia. I returned to Shandia. I did the things that presented themselves to me as duties each day, and in the doing of these I learned to know God a little better. To obey is to know. To know is to be at peace. I had no idea what the future might hold. It seemed impossible that I could continue the entire management of the Quichua station alone, but there was no use concerning myself with the next day. I was confident that, as in the case of the waterfowl,

> There is a Power whose care
> Teaches thy way along the pathless coast—
> The desert and illimitable air—
> Lone wandering, but not lost.
> . . . .
> He who, from zone to zone,
> Guides through the boundless sky thy certain flight,
> In the long way that I must tread alone,
> Will lead my steps aright.[1]

There was much maintenance work to oversee on the station: the clearing of weeds on the airstrip, the planting of pineapples and bananas, the constant work to keep the jungle back from the trails and clearings, the mending of fences and thatched roofs, the finishing of a school building which Jim had started, besides the ordinary work of living without many conveniences. I had a baby to care for, medical work to do among the Indians, a girls' school to teach, the translation of Quichua Scriptures to do, a Bible class in the boys' school to prepare for, and the shepherd-

---

[1] "To a Waterfowl" by William Cullen Bryant.

ing of a group of young Quichua Christians.

While I was at Shandia, the men of the Missionary Aviation Fellowship continued the flights begun over the Auca settlement by Nate Saint, who had been killed with my husband and the others. Gifts were dropped to the Aucas regularly, and the signs of friendship which they had given before the killing seemed unchanged. Many people, in all parts of the world, prayed for the Aucas, that the Light of the knowledge of God would somehow be taken to them. The odds against this seemed even greater now than they had before an attempt was made. But to know God is to trust Him, and we expected Him to do whatever might be necessary to open the Auca tribe. There were speculations as to how it might be done. Many people professed to know what mistakes the five men had made which led to their death. Psychologists and anthropologists wrote to explain what rules ought to be observed on the next attempt. Someone sent me sixty dollars with the request that it be used to buy Bibles for the Aucas. One lady asked that the Ten Commandments be written down on a slip of paper and dropped from the airplane to the Indians. Some said that if women were to go into the tribe they would be accepted. Others said this would be more dangerous than the five men going in, as women would be taken as common wives. Suggestions gleaned from encyclopedias, seances, Greek mythology, and Freudian psychology poured in.

It was clear to me that the central issue was not one of methods. Something could go wrong with the very best plan. Some unexpected factor could throw off the wisest calculations. I simply asked the Lord to do what He wanted to do about it. For once in my life I had no suggestions to make to Him about how He was to do it. I placed myself in His hands, saying that if He wanted to give me a part in reaching the Aucas, I was ready. I had noticed throughout the Bible that, when God asked a man to do something, methods, means, materials, and specific directions were always provided. The man had one thing to do: obey. This would have to be the only thing that mattered with regard to the Aucas. The words of Balaam in the Old Testament story seemed particularly appropriate: "Though Balak were to give me his house full of silver and gold, I could not go beyond the command of the

Lord my God, to do less or more."

But clearly the command for me to go had not been given, and unless I stuck to the job which *had* been given, I could not expect to recognize new guidance if it should come.

The Indians whom Jim had taught were learning to take more and more of the responsibilities in the Shandia church. One of the signs of health was an increasing interest on their part in Indians who had had no opportunity to hear of Jesus Christ. The death of the missionaries had awakened some of them to the seriousness of life, and they were praying more earnestly that God would send His Word to others. They began to make short trips to nearby points where missionaries had never been. They took over all of the preaching and most of the teaching in Shandia, and there was renewed interest in the translations of Scripture which were being printed for them.

Another missionary couple came to Shandia, and after a few months of language study they decided that they would stay there in the Quichua work. All these developments contributed to my conviction that I was to move on, perhaps out of the Quichua work and, although it seemed absurd, into the Auca work. I was certain that, if this was the case, it would be unmistakably clear *when the time came.*

One day in May, 1957, Johnny Keenan, the missionary pilot, asked me if I would like to accompany him on the flight to drop gifts to the Aucas. I had flown over the Auca village only once, and we had seen no people that time. This time we flew over three different locations where there were houses and manioc patches. At one of these I felt sure I saw "George," the young man who with two women had befriended Jim and the others a few days before they were killed. I had seen pictures of him which Nate Saint had taken. "George" grabbed the package we dropped to him and immediately started to eat the hamburger and bun, waving the streamers from the package so that we

> "Who will bring me to the fortified city? . . . Wilt not Thou,
> O God? O grant us help against the foe, for vain is the help
> of man!"

would be sure to see that he had got it. He ran from one side of the river to the other so as to be closer to us each time we buzzed the clearing. He raised his arms in what appeared to me to be a pleading gesture, and smiled and shouted. I could not help hoping that we might have to make a forced landing in that valley, so strong was the desire to meet the Aucas face to face. I understood then the eagerness of the five men to get down where they were. Yet at the same time there was a shrinking from the darkness and doom which they seemed to represent. I thought of the story of Ananias in Damascus, who, when the Lord spoke his name, said, "Here I am." The Lord gave the orders—to go and speak to a man named Saul—and Ananias reminded Him of Saul's reputation: a killer. But the Lord said, "Go." Ananias got up and went right into the house where he was. The dangers, public opinion, and prudence were quite irrelevant when the command was explicit. I was sure God could be trusted to make it as explicit to me, too.

In October, 1957, a hut which had been built on the Curaray River by an English missionary, Dr. Wilfred Tidmarsh, was sacked by the Aucas. The door was ripped off, his belongings were torn and scattered about, two lances were placed crosswise outside the door, and machetes and pots were stolen. Any hopes that the Aucas might be ready for another friendly approach were destroyed. It was clearer than ever that if anything was to be successful, it would have to be of God.

"Who will bring me to the fortified city? . . . Wilt not Thou, O God? O grant us help against the foe, for vain is the help of man! With God we shall do valiantly; it is he who will tread down our foes" (Psalm 60).

It was only a month after the attack on Dr. Tidmarsh's hut that the "miracle" we had expected occurred. I had been invited to the Tidmarshes' home in Arajuno. The decision to accept or not—ordinarily one I would have made quickly and without much difficulty—struck me this time as being rather an important one. I prayed about it and asked especially that I should not make a mistake. The answer was a strong affirmative—I should go. I had not been there a week when we received word that three Auca women had appeared at a Quichua settlement within walking distance of Arajuno.

2

The Gate of The Lord

ACCORDING TO EXPECTATION, when the time came to do something, the guidance was unmistakable. I knew that I was to go immediately with the Quichuas to meet the Auca women. The problem of whether or not to take my two-year-old Valerie, one which had caused me no small concern as I thought about an entrance into Aucaland, was solved for me—there was no one available to carry her, and Mrs. Tidmarsh kindly offered to take care of her for me. I had only a few minutes in which to collect equipment, as it was nearly noon and I knew the journey would take me about six hours. Night falls quickly in tropical forests.

I filled a small Indian carrying-net with notebooks, pencils, snake-bite kit, soap, a change of clothes, a light blanket, and insect repellent. My camera went into a waterproof bag, and we were soon on the trail. The two Indian guides asked me three or four times in the first mile or so if I was quite sure I could make it. They feared that this was my first attempt on a jungle trail and could probably picture themselves having to carry me the last few miles.

The first few miles were an old Shell Oil Company road, laid with stones but heavily overgrown with thorns and brush. The bridges were long since washed away, necessitating some steep descents into ravines. Beyond the Oglán River, a tributary of the Curaray, the trail was like any other jungle trail—wide enough for a single file, following the ridges as much as possible, to avoid the mud in the low places; up hills and down slippery banks, breaking out here and there onto a rock beach where the Indians danced lightly along from one smooth rock to another; crossing and recrossing streams and rivers where we waded sometimes ankle-deep, sometimes up to the thighs or even the waist. Now and again my guides stopped and pointed to a hollow in the bush, or a place where the undergrowth was slightly flattened.

"Look there, Señora. There is where an Auca has been watching. They hide by the trail and watch for us to pass. Look, here at the top of this cliff—here is where they wait to drop their spears on us as we climb. We saw their footprints here last week. It was only God who saved us."

I laughed. "It is only where a wild pig has slept!"

"A wild pig! A wild *pig*, she says! She doesn't know anything. We know. We have lived here. It is the Aucas, Señora. They walk all around. They know our territory."

Of course they might be right. The fact that the three Auca women were at the Curaray made it seem even more likely that Auca men might be watching us. I thought of Jim as I walked along behind the two Indians. Maybe I was on the same road, figuratively, that he had taken. And strangely, a simple spiritual that I had heard somewhere came to me just then: "I won't have to cross Jordan alone."

When we arrived at the Curaray River, where the Quichua settlement was, we found two Auca women—the third one had returned to the tribe—dressed by this time in a loose checked blouse and straight navy-blue skirt which is the usual Quichua outfit. They were surrounded by the entire community, apparently quite at home, until they caught a glimpse of me. They were terrified, and clutched tightly the hands of two old Quichua grandmothers who had taken them under their wing. I kept my distance for a time, talking with the Quichuas so that the Auca women might see that I was their friend. They looked me up and down, and finally when I approached them with a smile and attempted to touch their hands they loosened their grip on the other women and grinned faintly. I recognized one of them as being the older of the two women who had met my husband and the other men on "Palm Beach." I had seen pictures of the three Aucas, and this woman was unmistakable because her earlobe had been torn in an unusual way.

Knowing that the Aucas had stayed only a day on "Palm Beach" with the five men, I thought it likely that these two women would do the same, and I wanted to obtain as much language material as possible while they remained with us. I began immediately jotting down whatever I could of what they said, and they soon began to cooperate by giving me words when I said one of the few Auca phrases I knew: "What is this?" I had learned a few words before Jim had gone in to the Aucas. He and I met an Auca woman, Dayuma, who had escaped her tribe ten or twelve years before. She was a slave on a hacienda not far from Shandia at that time. Later she went on a visit to the United States with Rachel Saint, the sister of the pilot who was killed with Jim and the others.

In between language data I made notes on general observations: their eyebrows were plucked out completely; the hair was either shaved or plucked from their temples, cut in bangs straight across from ear to ear, hanging long in back; they had brought only one thing in their hands when they came out—a new packet of matches which had been dropped to them from the plane. They gave this to me. They seemed to know the use of matches but were afraid to strike them. I showed them my flashlight without out lighting it, remembering that the men had dropped a flashlight to them earlier and wondering if they had understood it. They showed no comprehension, so I turned it on for them, to their great delight. They enjoyed listening to the ticking of my watch, though neither made a comment. The Quichuas joined the game and offered them homemade cigarettes. Mankamu (I did not learn their names for weeks afterwards) was bold enough to try a smoke, but spat disgustedly on the ground and handed the cigarette back. They tried salt, registered neither pleasure nor distaste, and said nothing. They gave me a word for "gun" and pantomimed how a gun was used to kill animals and/or people (I could not be sure which they meant).

When night came they indicated that they wanted to sleep, and were shown into a tiny bamboo-walled room where they lay down quite contentedly between the two old Quichua women. Some of the Quichuas began to sing, and I joined them. This brought broad grins from the Aucas. When we had sung, Mankamu obliged, without any invitation, by singing one of her own songs. It consisted of a single note, apparently no words, or perhaps a series of vowels, with emphasis thus: —. —. —. —. —. This continued for so long that the Quichuas began to grow uneasy. "She is singing to cast a spell!" they said. "And then her people will attack us!" They stood their guns and lances up beside them where they slept, and each time the dogs stirred or barked, the men leaped to their feet. "Aucas!" Many took it for granted that the women were a decoy, as they supposed the Aucas had been who befriended the five missionaries. They were supposed to gain our confidence and then open the way for an all-out attack by the men of the Auca tribe. This was a possibility, but it did not change my certainty that God had brought me to that place. He was to me that night, as the Psalmist said, a "strong tower."

At four-thirty the next morning Mankamu woke the household with her strange chanting. There was much speculation as to whether this was singing, crying, or spell-casting. She appeared to be ill, and soon was shaking with chills. I offered her a malaria remedy, and she took the pills without hesitation, swallowing them whole with a gulp of water. I was amazed. The pills were exceedingly bitter. How did she know I was not trying to kill her?

The day passed slowly. The Quichuas worked for an hour or two, then returned to the house and sat somewhat restlessly, apprehensive of a surprise attack by Aucas. It was very hot, and the clouds of flies, the smell of termite-nest smoke (used to discourage the flies), the misery of sitting on a tiny block of wood with my knees under my chin, the absence of a cup of coffee, not to mention the absence of my child, all helped to dissipate any feeling of romance which might have dominated the scene from a distance. The Indians passed the time in the usual way—the women cooked, men sat and twiddled a stick, picked at an old violin, killed flies with a wooden paddle, picked scabs. When the food was ready they squatted around a banana leaf on the ground and ate: the ubiquitous manioc, accompanied by fish and peccary meat.

Shortly after noon the dogs barked, and the men grabbed guns and rushed to the manioc patch to investigate. They found twigs of the manioc freshly broken off with the milk still running. Someone had been there. There were no other Indians within twelve miles. It had to be Aucas. "They are spying on us," they said. "They will look to see if we have killed their two women. If they do not see them, they will kill us." I had been considering asking the women to go back to Arajuno with me, where we could live in some comfort and would be farther away from the apparent danger on the Curaray. But it appeared now that the dangers would be greater to the Indians if I should leave, and so I began to make plans to remain in the Quichua settlement. The two Aucas were apparently quite happy with their newfound "mothers," and it seemed a wise thing to settle there with them, where they would be in an Indian environment and where I could study their language.

Dr. Tidmarsh arrived that afternoon with a tape recorder. Mankamu watched his demonstration for a moment, then calmly took the microphone and spoke. Her talk was of killings, spears, and of her child who had just died. She was amused, though not dumbfounded, when her voice was played back to her. The following day the airplane flew over and brought a telephone. Circling slowly the plane let the line down to where I stood. I caught the telephone as it reached the vortex and talked with the pilots as they continued to circle. Mintaka, one of the Auca women, showed not the slightest interest in either plane or telephone. Mankamu seemed to be afraid, and talked excitedly all during the time the plane circled.

Sunday is the Quichua feast day, and the Indians dressed in feathers and paint for a drink-and-dance. The two Aucas showed only mild amusement at this spectacle. Mankamu accompanied the drumming by chanting, not necessarily in time to the drumbeat. When the *chicha* was served—the manioc beer which is the Indians' food-drink but is fermented for a longer time for a feast—the Quichuas followed their usual custom of sipping some and refusing the rest in the gourd. Mankamu and Mintaka followed their own custom of drinking the bowl dry, not realizing that it was highly intoxicating. Mankamu soon complained of a headache, and Mintaka found she could not retain the several quarts of liquid she had taken on.

I was pleased to find that the Quichua men treated both the women with complete respect. Mintaka angered some of the women by flirting quite openly with the men. I did not know at the time that she was a "grass widow" and perhaps would have been happy to gain a husband from outside her own tribe, since the Auca male population was badly depleted.

A few days later, more convinced than ever that the Curaray village was the place for the Auca women and me to stay, I went out to Shandia to pack my things for the move. The Indians had promised to build me a small house and were already clearing ground for it when I left. The two women seemed to have made up their minds to stay, though for what reason was a mystery to me. I could not get so much as a syllable of what they said most of the time. It was evident, however, that they were not afraid.

In Shandia I reviewed the steps that had led to this apparent opening into the Auca tribe. I had prayed for the opening. I had not known how it could happen. God had done the impossible and made two *women*—not men—come out, just when I was within reach, and had enabled me to meet them and gain some measure of their confidence. The words of Psalm 118 were a special help as I contemplated what the move to the Curaray might mean.

"I do not fear what man can do unto me. . . . The Lord is on my side to help me.

"It is better to take refuge in the Lord than to put confidence in man.

"The Lord is my Strength and Song.

"I shall not die, but I shall live, and recount the deeds of the Lord.

"This is the gate of the Lord; the righteous enter through it.

"This is the Lord's doing. It is marvelous in our eyes. . . . O Lord, we beseech Thee, give us success. . . . Blessed be he that enters in the name of the Lord.

"The Lord is God, and He has given us light.

"Thou art my God, and I will give thanks to Thee."

I had known a very few times in my life when I had not a prop to lean on, no hint of which course to take, no one from whom to ask advice. This was such a time, and in answer to prayer these words, written so long ago, under such different conditions, came to me with such unshakable assurance that I had to believe they were written for me. They were the voice of God. I seized them, acted on them, and in acting discovered the Rock beneath.

So we went, Valerie in a little wooden chair made by Fermín, the Quichua Christian who carried her, and I on foot. Another Quichua accompanied us to carry our gear. Valerie had never been on a long trip in the jungle trail before, but the gentle motion of the chair rocked her to sleep several times. The pouring rain woke her in late afternoon, but she was a good sport about it, a real little Indian, and did not complain. I was impressed with the skill Fermín showed in carrying her. It was quite a trick to slide underneath fallen trees, climb slippery cliffs, negotiate through high thorns without bumping Val's head or scraping her off the chair. At one point, in crossing a stream, Fermín slipped on a rock. He fell, twisting his foot rather badly, but held himself in such a way that Val was still upright and uninjured.

We reached the Curaray just at dusk, having taken eight and a half hours for the trip because of the relentless rain which made running rivers of the trails. Mankamu and Mintaka were still there and seemed to understand that I had brought my child because I planned to stay there with them.

The following morning we women—Quichuas, Aucas, white woman and child—were all bathing in the river after the men had gone off on the hunt. Suddenly a cry came from the house across the river: "Aucas!" Every house in the settlement came alive at once and someone shouted, "They've already killed! Honorio is dead! Get out of the river, Señora, quick. *Aucas are coming!*" Although the name Auca is a Quichua word, Mintaka and Mankamu seemed immediately to apprehend what had happened.

Dario, the sole man in the village at the time, came running downriver with his shotgun, heading for the scene of the murder. Mankamu followed, shouting as she went. Mintaka sat stolidly on the beach, while I frantically tried to dress and decide where to go. We were in the most vulnerable position possible if it was actually true that Aucas were about to attack. But to run to the house would mean that we were closer to the forest, from which they might issue at any moment. Since Mintaka was sitting so calmly on the rocks nearby, I decided to stay with her. When no one returned from the scene, we finally went back to the house. The mother of Honorio, the dead man, ran by weeping, saying, "We'll die together. If they kill me, I will die with my son." I debated going with her. The thought of Valerie stopped me. I had made up my mind when I brought her that I would take no unnecessary risks. It was necessary that I come this far, and bring her into whatever danger living there might mean. It was not necessary to go downriver closer to where the Aucas had appeared. It was at least possible that they might be lurking near the scene.

Later the Quichuas returned with the body of the dead man. Eighteen spears were removed, one of them wrapped with the pages of a New Testament which the Aucas had probably stolen from Dr. Tidmarsh's hut when they raided it. Another was decorated with the cloth used to make a scrapbook which Mrs. Tidmarsh had sent to be dropped to them from the airplane. The

The coming of Mintaka and Mankamu, two Auca women, changed again the course of my life.

"My son, my baby, my baby! You went out to hunt this morning alive and beautiful. They got you—the demons, the animals, those demons the Aucas!" Melchiora wails the death wail. The Quichuas had been apprehensive because of the presence of two Aucas in their community, but hopeful at the same time that at last the enmity was gone. Their fears were justified—Honorio was found one morning bristling with eighteen spears, his wife carried away by the killers.

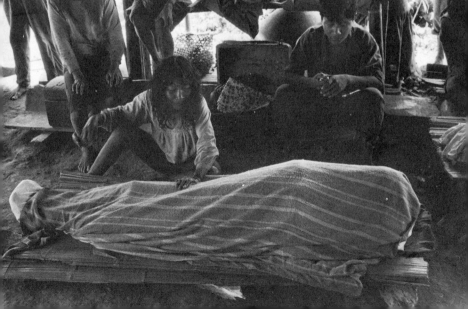

spears appeared to be new, or at least newly decorated, and all were more or less bloody. "A thousand shall fall at thy side, and ten thousand at thy right hand, but it shall not come nigh thee" entered my mind as I looked at the sheaf of weapons. Valerie played around, put a basin on her head, said, "Hat, Mama," and asked where her dolly was.

We went over to Honorio's house where his mother and brother lay weeping and caressing the still form wrapped in an old cotton blanket. His wife was nowhere to be found. She had been with him when they started downriver to hunt or fish for the day. They found his canoe, the remains of some *chicha*, and his dog dead on the sand, with three spears protruding from its back. Maruja, the teen-age wife, had undoubtedly been carried away captive by the killers. Mankamu seemed to be indicating to me that that is what they would do to Valerie—they would kill me and carry her away. She made a long, loud, and very excited speech to the mourners when she saw the body. No one understood a word. She began to tremble, and there were tears in her eyes. The screaming wail of the Quichua women, rising in pitch and intensity each time a newcomer arrived, and the growing suspense when the men did not return from their day's hunting contributed to a high tension. Dario asked me if I was afraid. No. "They will carry you away, too," he said. At that moment the wind blew over the pages of my Bible, which lay open on my lap. "I know that Thou canst do all things, and that no purpose of Thine can be thwarted" was the sentence that caught my eye. Did I believe this? I felt, for a short time, that I had had enough of the Aucas. I would have been very glad to get out of the jungle, away from all that it meant.

The Quichua men began to return, one by one, from the hunt. They had had no inkling of the presence of Aucas, or of the killing of Honorio. When the last one, Donasco, arrived, he was pale and frightened. He had heard Aucas, he said, and hid in a tree. About ten yards from him six Aucas passed through the underbrush, with a young boy, he thought, in the middle. When he heard the story of the killing, he surmised that the "boy" must have been Maruja. They argued about the motivation.

"It is because you people drop them gifts. They don't want

them. You ought to drop bombs, not gifts," said one of the women to me.

"They kill because Dr. Tidmarsh built a house here. They do not want the white man. They see you here, and they come to kill."

Then there was an argument between those who believed that if we should leave, the Aucas would think we had killed the two women, and those who thought that if we did not leave, the Aucas would be angry on account of our presence.

Bili, one of the old grandmothers, quietly begged me to stay, to "keep them company." "The men will build you a house, Señora. We want you to stay." Her son Dario was silent.

"They will kill, and keep on killing, now that they have begun," said one.

"No, they never kill twice in the same place. They will not come back," said another.

I tried to find out what Mankamu was thinking. I gestured toward Arajuno. "No," she said. I caught the words "my child, remembering."

"The Aucas like to kill," said one man. "They kill for sport. They are playing."

"Then let them come here," Dario put in. "We'll play with *them*."

I found peace in the knowledge that I was in the hands of God. Not in the confidence that I was not going to be killed. Not in any false sense of security that God would protect me, any more than He protected my husband, the four missionaries, or Honorio from the wooden lances. Simply in knowing that He held my destiny in His two hands, and that what He did was right.

The following morning the decision to leave the Curaray village was clear. Mankamu willingly went with us to Arajuno, leaving Mintaka behind to follow with the other Indians when they evacuated the site a few days later. Neither woman had any idea what lay before her, yet neither consulted the other about her plans. Indeed, when Mankamu left, Mintaka did not bother to come down from the second floor to bid her good-by or to ask where she was going.

Within a week, however, we met again in Arajuno and flew to

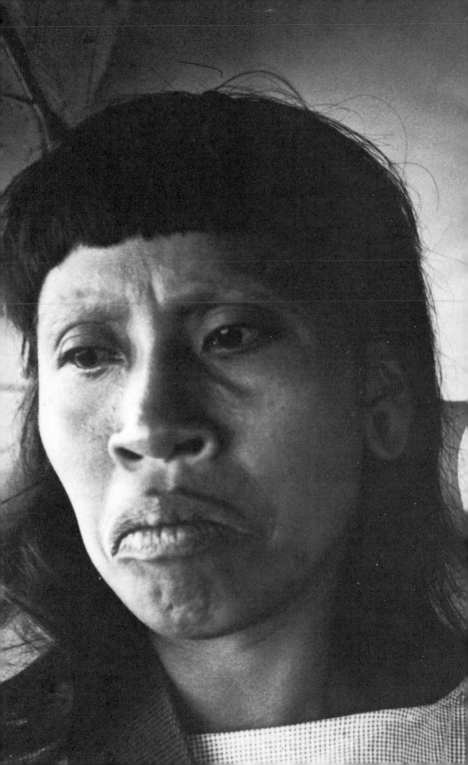

Shandia, where Indian friends had invited us to live with them. I explained to Mankamu as best I could that we were going for a ride in a plane. She seemed to understand, and ordered Mintaka to get in first. Mintaka did nothing without orders from Mankamu. She got in somewhat hesitantly, followed by Mankamu, who, when the pilot strapped her into the safety belt, issued instructions to Mintaka to do the same with her belt. The roar of the engine frightened them so that they covered their heads with blankets, but it was not long before curiosity overcame them and they peeped out to watch the landscape below.

3

Mintaka and Mankamu— "They're Just Indians"

WHEN WE ARRIVED in Shandia Mintaka and Mankamu again were the center of attention for some days. Indians and whites came from miles around to see these genuine Aucas. The remarks indicated the kind of reputation Aucas had gained for themselves—something other than human.

"Why, they're just like us! They're just Indians!"

"Do they eat? Do they speak? This last question was answered by one of the spectators before I had a chance: "No, stupid. But they do make sounds, don't they, Señora?"

"And they have only two legs! I had thought they had about six, but I just counted them and there were only two." This from one of the Shandia schoolboys.

We were welcomed into the home of a family of Indian believers in Shandia. A bamboo bed was fixed for Mintaka and Mankamu in the central room, next to the fire. I was given a corner of a bedroom occupied by a married couple. In a short time the Indians had built an addition onto the house where I had a tiny kitchen, study, and space for Valerie's bed.

Language study began in earnest then. Rachel Saint sent me some data which helped greatly in the fundamentals of the grammar. She had been working for several years on the Auca language with Dayuma. The tape which Mankamu had made for Dr. Tidmarsh was sent to Dayuma and Rachel, who were in the United States, and they translated it for us. I learned that Mankamu's daughter had died. This had led her to want to leave home and visit the foreigners. The information on the tape also furnished enough clues for Dayuma to tell us the names of the two women. Both of them proved to be her aunts. When Dayuma made a tape for Mankamu and Mintaka, I played it for them and simultaneously recorded their comments and answers to Dayuma's questions, which in turn I sent to her. She learned that her mother, Akawu, was still alive but her favorite brother had been killed years before.

Though Mankamu and Mintaka shared in the normal work of the Quichua household—going to the plantation and weeding manioc in order to get their share of food—they had no other responsibilities and consequently spent most of their time stretched out on the bamboo bed. It served as a psychiatrist's couch. I found that if I sat down beside them with pen and pad Mankamu would soon begin talking. She gave no evidence of realizing that I did not understand a word she said. She would talk at full speed, often with a mouth full of manioc, and nearly always with her back turned, facing the wall. I would sometimes lean over her in order to see her mouth, because I could not correctly record a sound on paper unless I could see how it was produced. But even seeing her mouth, which had very few teeth to begin with, proved little help if it was upside down, or full. Often she would whisper, telling a story of a killing, lest the Indians overhear her. Because the Quichuas used the affirmative grunt common to both languages, the women were perfectly sure that everything they said was understood. The fact that they themselves could not understand the Quichua language had nothing

There were no language barriers between Mintaka and Valerie.

to do with it. I had learned earlier that Indians generally regard their own language as universal. To be sure, there were others who did not speak it, but surely they must "*hear*" it—anyone could understand *their* language. When I asked them—even educated Quichuas—if they understood English, they replied, "Well, anyone can see that *that* language is not hearable. But our language—oh, that's different. Everyone can understand that." So I supposed that the Aucas held the same view. When I repeated the phrase I had learned well: "I do not understand," they sometimes became quite annoyed with me. "You *do* understand. You are just talking nonsense!" (The last was a word I had learned from Rachel's vocabulary list.)

There were times when my two charges tried desperately to tell me something they wanted. It was agony. I was eager to give them all they needed, and every possible comfort, but my ignorance of the kind of life they had come from made it difficult to guess at anything more than I had already provided. I had judged their wants in the only way I knew—from experience with Quichuas. They seemed to eat the same things, cook them in the same way, plant and gather them in the same way. So whenever I was aware that something was lacking, I did everything I could to discover what it was, often without success. Mintaka would take this as a personal offense and went for days without speaking to anyone. She would sit in high dudgeon on the edge of the bamboo bed and snort at anyone who approached her. Mankamu seemed to comprehend my difficulty and continued to try to make me understand. Though very adept in the use of gestures as an accompaniment to ordinary conversation, she did not use them as a substitute when I failed to respond to a word which she was shouting and repeating.

In spite of my annoying ignorance both women accepted me with a good-natured tolerance most of the time and occasionally showed themselves quite affectionate. Mintaka enjoyed playing with Valerie, tickling her and teasing her as mothers do with children. But then she was often impatient with her, at times to the point of slapping her. Mankamu, on the other hand, while never openly affectionate to her, was never impatient. She would carry her piggyback on the jungle trails or give orders to Mintaka to do so. Whenever they went to the river to bathe or fish, Valerie went with them. They shared their food with her when she went to "watch them eat," as she said. She preferred Indian food to my cooking and had learned that, even though she was not allowed to ask for it, if she went and "watched," she was given something.

I continued to do some of the medical work of the Shandia station, and when I was asked to give an injection I made it a point to take Mintaka and Mankamu with me so that they could observe the process, in case they should ever need an injection. I wanted them to see that the Indians asked to be punctured with a needle, and of course I hoped that they would understand the relation between the medicine and the cure. They thought it terribly funny to watch the sick person wince, but a few weeks later, when Mankamu developed a rather bad case of bronchitis, the doctor prescribed penicillin. I showed her the bottle and the needle, and she pushed up her sleeve without hesitation.

One night I heard Mankamu crying. I went out to the fireplace, where she was sitting holding a glowing stick close to her badly swollen cheek. I caught the word "tooth" in what she said. The next day I arranged for a flight to take her out to the army dentist in the little town of Shell Mera. She and Mintaka apparently knew the purpose of the journey and began packing up all their worldly goods—combs, mirrors, pot, colored beads, etc.

"Shall we take our pots? Shall we take the blanket?" When I had said no to these questions, I had difficulty persuading them to take a change of clothing. That was the last thing an Auca would think necessary.

This time there was no difficulty in getting them into the airplane. They enjoyed the flight out, and when they saw the pickup truck waiting to take them to the dentist, although it was the first vehicle they had ever seen besides the plane, they hopped right in. At the dentist's office Mankamu obediently got into the chair indicated and submitted to needles in the face and the yanking of four molars, leaving her with two which were still whole. Mintaka settled herself on the floor by the chair, laughing behind her hand when the dentist tossed the offending teeth into the corner. Mankamu trembled with pain but made no sound of complaint. She could see some sense in the process, which unfortunately was not the case later on when I wanted to have the two women X-rayed. The machine was an old model, and the plate had to be held just so by the patient. It was quite a struggle getting them to copy my demonstration—hold their chins up, put their elbows forward, stand still, and take deep breaths! Mintaka simply refused, until Mankamu realized that we were serious in wanting them to imitate us, and she gave Mintaka orders to obey. Both of them moved, however, and we had to repeat the foolishness the following day, much to their disgust. The tests for tuberculosis proved negative, and the doctor's physical examination, to which they submitted without question, showed them to be strong and healthy.

As we walked down the road in Shell Mera a truck came lurching and roaring toward us. Grabbing up Valerie, the women plunged for the ditch, willing to let me die if I chose but determined to rescue Val. When the truck rolled on by and I was unscathed, they emerged giggling and sheepish. The sight of a mule was a shock to them, especially when it made no move to escape, as the animals they knew would have done. But the sound of a donkey braying and the spectacle of a man on horseback nearly gave them hysterics—the first of fear, the second of amusement.

One of my earliest encouragements in the language study came on the morning we were to return to Shandia from Shell Mera. I had tried to explain to the two women that we were to spend one more night, and then, in the morning, we would get into the plane and go back to our house. I was not at all sure that they understood me. They nearly always grunted in a way which meant "Is that so?" whenever I spoke to them. So I was elated to find, next morning, that they had their carrying-nets all packed and were sitting on the bed waiting for me.

A few weeks later I was encouraged again: Mankamu actually made an effort to help me learn the language. Until that time she and Mintaka had seemed to assume that I knew it all, and neither would repeat things they said, or had any idea of speaking slowly so that I could understand. We were on the trail one day when we came upon two men weaving a thatched roof. Mankamu said, "What are they doing?" She smiled. It was obvious that she knew what they were doing. She wanted me to tell her in her own language! I said I did not know, and she immediately gave me the correct dual form (Auca has duals, e.g., "we two, you two," as well as plurals: "we, you") of the verb "to weave" and then even waited for me to repeat it. This, I felt, was real progress.

Then there were the times of keenest interest to me, when they described their observations of the five missionary men. Mintaka found a large straw hat hanging on my wall. She put it on, and leaned over the edge of the bed, calling out in Auca, with American intonations, such things as "We like you. We will give you gifts." Suddenly I realized that she was imitating Pete Fleming, who had worn a straw hat and had called out to the Aucas from the airplane. On another occasion when they were in Shell Mera, Mankamu went up into the attic with me to examine the lances I had collected at the time of the killing of the Quichua Honorio. She knew who had made each one by the type of carving and bird feathers used. Then, seeing a small window at the end of the attic, she went over and put her head out, calling out phrases which she had probably heard shouted by the pilots who flew over their settlement after January, 1956. I showed her a basket in which Nate Saint had received a live parrot. "I made that," she said. She described how she had woven it, how Akawu had furnished the string with which to tie it, another had given a piece of barkcloth to wrap around it, and Minkayi had donated his pet parrot. When the men dropped the spiraling line, they had all gathered around excitedly and tied the big bundle onto it. Seeing it safely pulled up into the sky gave Nampa, one of the young men, an idea. Next time it came he tied the line around his own waist. "I'll go with the foreigners," he had said. But Nate had purposely arranged a break-cord in case the Aucas should tie on too heavy a load. Nampa was disappointed.

There were other times when my ignorance of the language was especially galling. I took the women to visit Umi, an Auca woman who lived on a hacienda not far from Shandia. I gave them no warning of where we were going, but they recognized her immediately, though it had been many years since they saw her. She too had left the tribe, and having lived with Quichuas all during that time had forgotten her Auca to a large extent. Though she could understand what they said to her, she became hopelessly confused trying to answer, and I soon found myself having to interpret from her mixed-up Quichua, into my mixed-up Auca, so that Mintaka and Mankamu could understand!

When I showed the women the colored slides which the pilot, Nate Saint, had taken of the three Aucas—Mintaka, Gimari, and Naenkiwi—on "Palm Beach" they showed little amazement, and I scarcely understood what they did say, but they made it clear to me that Gimari ("Delilah") was Dayuma's younger sister, and that Naenkiwi ("George") was now dead. Thus bit by bit I gleaned information about which we had wondered for a long time.

In the spring I took them to Ecuador's most modern city, the port of Guayaquil. I was warned of fearful risks—their being kidnaped, or contracting some fatal white man's disease—but I felt it important that when they returned to their own people, which they often talked of doing, they should be able to tell them firsthand something of the foreigners' world. We traveled by bus, jeep, and train, up over the 12,000-foot pass of the Andes, where they were greatly impressed with the cold, and down the steep western slope to the coastal plain. Guayaquil, with its modern buildings, cars, ferryboats, neon lights, and broad paved streets, held little of interest to the two women except an outdoor market. When they saw the block-long stacks of bananas they gasped. "Who can possibly have cut all those bananas for one day? Whoever will eat them?" They were beside themselves with delight when I took them to the fish market and told them to take whatever they liked. From the bewildering array of salt-water fish they chose two kinds which resembled foods they were accustomed to—live crabs and crayfish. These they turned loose under the bed in their room, except for the ones they roasted over a kerosene flame to eat immediately. It was in Guayaquil that they had opportunity to see, for the first time, the colored movie footage of Mintaka, Gimari, and Naenkiwi, which Nate had made. They giggled, and Mintaka became properly coy when her own image was thrown on the screen, but apart from that they were quite blasé. Mintaka even got bored, said she had a headache, and wandered out of the room before the film was finished. Mankamu, however, explained to us what they were doing, who they were. She was quite pleased at being able thus to spy on Gimari's behavior with Naenkiwi, who was not at that time her husband!

I had hoped the Guayaquil trip would be a fruitful one from the standpoint of language work. I had taken along my notebook, of course, but found that the women made very few comments. In checking over the data I discovered one word which recurred frequently. It was given in answer to questions about sierra flora, about the snow-capped mountains, goats, sheep, and rabbits. I had not noticed, until later, that I was getting the same word for all of these—I had assumed that the words I elicited would lead to some interesting similarity in their experience, though I knew of course that the objects named were new to them. Further checking revealed that the utterance meant simply "Who knows *what* it is!

Progress in the language was so painfully slow, and moments of illumination were so rare, that I often felt discouraged. On one of these mornings I asked God especially to help me to understand something specific in what the women said to me.

I went into the big central room where they had their bamboo bed, and sat down with pen and notebook. Mankamu began to talk of her home and children. Her children were still alive when she left. She had promised them she would return. The time had come—she wanted to go back and see them.

"You will go with us, Gikari. [She used the name Mintaka had given me: 'Woodpecker.' I could not get to the bottom of her reason for this.] We will go in the airplane to the doctor's [Tidmarsh's] house. From there we will go on foot. We know the trail. We will carry Valerie. We will live with Gikita [Mankamu's husband, Mintaka's brother]. He will fish for us and bring us meat from the forest. We will have a good house—the roof won't leak like this one. There will be plenty of plantain and manioc, but if you want, the plane can drop your food for you. We will help you pick it up. You will see our children. They are this age [pointing to several children in the room]. They will love you and your child. You will take your [hypodermic] needle and help the sick people. We will all live well."

"But they will spear us, won't they?" I asked.

"It is the downriver ones who spear. They are far away."

"But your people speared my husband. They will spear me."

"Gikari! Your husband was a *man! You are a woman!*"

"But what about Dabu and Munga? Will they not spear me?"

"Dabu is my kinsman! We will say, "Here is our mother. She is like Ipanai [Mintaka's mother]. We love her. She is good.""

It sounded convincing enough, especially since I wanted badly to be convinced. But in the small hours of the morning, as I lay awake thinking of what such a move could mean, I had to have far more than the word of an Auca woman. I asked the Lord for His word. It came, from the book of Nehemiah:

"Thou art the Lord. . . . Thou didst find his heart faithful and didst make with him a covenant to give to his descendants the land . . . and Thou hast fulfilled Thy promise, for Thou art righteous. . . . By a pillar of cloud Thou didst lead them in the day, and by a pillar of fire in the night to light for them the way in which they should go. . . . Thou gavest Thy good Spirit to instruct them. . . . Thou didst sustain them in the wilderness, and they lacked nothing. . . . Thou didst bring them into the land . . . and Thou didst subdue before them the inhabitants of the land."

He had done it for a people long ago. He could do this for us. I took the words literally, and thanked Him that He was going to take Valerie and me to the tribe with Mintaka and Mankamu.

The few who knew of this contemplated step wrote immediately to warn and question me. Some told me point-blank that I must be mistaken. To disregard completely what one called the "most elementary rules of prudence" would be folly. I certainly needed no stronger proof of the nature of the people I proposed to visit than their treatment of my husband. I knew that my position was quite indefensible. But I knew, too, that it was the duty which lay before me. That duty I took to be the will of God. I had heard no voices, seen no visions. But it seemed to me that the Bible, which I regard as a book of principles by which we

Sunshine, clear rivers, even a duck to play with—the little white girl had all she could ask.

are to live if we want to know what real freedom is, was daily presenting to me fresh confirmation of the fact that I had not mistaken God's design, and so I went ahead. One morning my Bible reading fell at the story of Queen Esther. Esther was well acquainted with the law which required that anyone entering the king's presence without being called should be killed. She knew, also, that it was her duty to go in to entreat the king's favor on behalf of her people. This illustrated again the principle: if a duty is clear, the dangers surrounding it are irrelevant.

At last I received the news I had been looking for: Rachel Saint and Dayuma were back in Ecuador and invited Mintaka, Mankamu, Valerie, and me to come to their jungle base and see them. I did not tell the two women where we were going, nor had I mentioned Dayuma's returning, but when they got out of the plane and saw her, Mintaka remarked simply, "That's Dayuma," and Mankamu launched into a rapid-fire account of all that had taken place since Dayuma had fled the tribe. Although Dayuma had heard from the tapes Mankamu had sent her that her two brothers had died, she wept to hear the news firsthand.

We spent about two months together—the three Auca women, Rachel, and I—working on the language. Then they decided it was time to return to their people.

"I promised them I would come back when the kapok is ripe. It is ripe now, Gikari. I am going home," Mankamu said. Then she made a tape for me, which, when laboriously translated, gave me more of the story:

"[When I get home] I'll say to my brother: 'Don't be afraid. We lived in Gikari's house. She was good. She will come to live here with us. We will make an airstrip. From now on you will not kill. God's Word says, "Don't fear. Don't lie." You must tell the others this. Tell them all of it. We will live well. This teaching, having learned, I come. Just think about food—don't think about

*Rachel Saint, sister of the pilot who was killed with my
husband and three fellow missionaries, talks with the Auca
women, using what she had learned in several years' study
with Dayuma.*

killing people. As the months pass you'll get to know Gikari. Don't be afraid of her.'

"[On the way down to our houses] we'll sleep at Añangu River. Next day we'll be on the trail still. On the third day we'll arrive.

" 'Men, brothers, fathers, people like our own relatives, will come to visit us here,' I'll say to my people. 'Don't fear them. Build Gikari's house. We will bring her here. Make also a guest house and an airstrip. When she is here, her friends will come to sleep sometimes. Collect pets and animals from the jungle. These you will give them in exchange for their gifts.'

"My people will say yes.

" 'When they come in the airplane, you'll see them. They'll take you for flights. I had rides in the plane. They will teach you God's words. You must listen and teach the children. Listen well—hear them sing. It is good, that which they teach.'

"We'll build our houses on the Lahuano River, on a nice open place. You and I will have houses side by side. I'll tell them to make a huge strip, cut down all the trees.

"Last night I dreamed I took some Quichua women down there, and told my relatives to cut them some wood!

"If I don't go home soon, I won't be able to find my family. They will move far away. They will wait till now, for this is the season of kapok. If I don't arrive before it passes, they'll leave.

"They may be living in small houses, separated throughout the forest. We would not be able to find their footprints. We ought to go while they are still together in one place. Then they will listen and say yes.

Rachel Saint and I compared notes on the language, the results of her study with Dayuma and mine with Mintaka and Mankamu. A filing system was the only way to analyze the data.

Dayuma, a Christian Auca woman who had left her people years before, translates for me into Quichua what Mintaka is saying. Mintaka felt at home in a palm-fiber hammock of the type woven by Auca women.

"I will say to Dabu [her brother], 'Remember how you cried when they killed the five foreigners? They were good men. You wished they had lived. The wife of one of them lives. She is good. She will come here to live. You must spear fish for us. From now on we will live happily. Things will be different. We won't cry any more.'

"I saw some *chonda* blossoms. This means it is time to go home. A year is nearly up. My children will not do well if I don't go to see them. They will think I am dead, and do what they please.

"Nimu [Rachel] said, 'You are still sick. You can't go now.' We said, 'We're fine. We better go while we're still well.'

"I'll tell my people to make you a house with a floor. I'll say 'Stop fearing the Quichuas. Fear only the downriver ones.' I'll make them all work, every one of them together, to build the house and airstrip.

" 'Believing in God, we'll live well. Lots of people we knew were believers,' I'll tell them. You too must become a believing group.' "

And so, one morning in September, we flew to Arajuno: Dayuma, Mintaka, Mankamu, three puppies, aluminum pots, knives and beads for the Aucas, and Valerie and I. The three women had decided by this time that they did not want me to accompany them into their tribe on the first visit. "You wait here at the doctor's house," Mankamu said. "You will live well with your Quichua friends. One day we will come back and take you with us to our home."

They set off down the airstrip, toward the jungle trail which had brought them out to civilization. We prayed with them, just before they left us at the edge of the forest. Dayuma prayed in the Auca tongue, and they disappeared among the trees. I wondered if we would ever see them again. Dayuma had not been certain her people would not want to kill her. Would they be angry at Mintaka and Mankamu for having stayed away so long?

A week later Dan Derr, the MAF pilot, and I flew over the Auca settlement to see if there were any signs of the three women. The Aucas seemed to be there, and I saw several dressed in clothes, but there was certainly no sign of Dayuma. One woman I saw appeared to be Mankamu. She jumped up and down, gesticulated wildly, and shouted. I noticed her pointing to a big man at her side. Was it Gikita, her husband? I shouted the things she had told me beforehand to shout: "I am Gikari. I have come. I see you. I am Gikari." Of course I called her name, and Mintaka's. I said, "Where is Dayuma? Where is Mintaka?" She gestured again, but so ambiguously that I could not interpret whether she was pointing out a direction, pantomiming a killing, or saying she did not know.

She had left a few trinkets with me which I dropped to her, so that those who were with her could be sure that I was, after all, Gikari, as she told them. Included in the little bundle was a picture of Mankamu, Mintaka, Valerie, and me.

We carefully searched all the houses, which were miles apart. There was no sign of the other two women. All those we saw were naked, and they had promised to be dressed. Dayuma had mentioned the "bucket-drop," which she understood, and said that she would speak on the telephone to me if we dropped it to her. We had it with us, hoping to be able to do this.

When we reached Arajuno again, the Quichuas received the news with long faces. "They'll all have been speared long ago. What makes you think you'll ever see them again?"

A few days later Dr. Tidmarsh and a friend made another visit to his little house on the Curaray, hoping perhaps to learn something of the women while they supervised the Indians who were working on an airstrip. They, too, returned without any news. When two weeks had passed we were seriously concerned. Dr. Tidmarsh and I made another flight to look for the women. No evidence. We realized that Dayuma might have gone to another location of which we knew nothing. It is no easy thing to locate an Auca hut in a small clearing, among so many hills and valleys. We learned later that she had gone to a spot where she had lived as a child, where there was no clearing at all, and sent word by Mankamu for the rest to come and meet her there. This was the reason for our not having located them. So we waited, asking God to protect them and bring them out in His time. We knew that His timing is perfect, and that He would do the very best thing for all.

4

"Take Me
to Mintaka's House"

O N SEPTEMBER 25, 1958, I was laying some clothes on the grass in the sun when three Quichua Indians arrived from the Curaray River.

"Good morning," I said. "Why have you come?"

"For no reason"—the stock answer to most questions, which we have learned to take with a grain of salt.

"Have you no word about the Auca women?"

"Oh. Yes—they came out."

Some prodding revealed that seven Auca women, including the three who had gone in, and three Auca boys were at the moment within a half-hour's walk of my house. I shouted to Marj Saint, who was staying with me at the time since the Tidmarshes had gone to Quito, and we started down the airstrip with Valerie and my camera. Just as we reached the end we heard someone singing "Jesus Loves Me" in English. I knew Dayuma's voice and poised my camera. Out of the high grass broke Dayuma, Mintaka, and Mankamu, followed by four women and two boys. Mankamu fell into my arms, burning with fever but apparently glad to see us, an emotion which she had rarely exhibited before.

Only one of the newcomers wore clothes—the skirt and blouse which Dayuma had given her. Clapping her on the shoulder and pulling her forward, Dayuma introduced her to us. "This is Ipa, one of the wives of Naenkiwi ['George']." Ipa came forward un-self-consciously and stood quietly. I was struck by the sweetness of her expression and the simplicity with which she watched us: this was the woman who had strangled her own child and buried her, still alive, with her husband when he had been speared by her brother.

The others were introduced in turn: Watu, Naenu, and Gakamu, all single girls; Kinta and Gingatae, boys of ten and twelve, the latter being Mintaka's son, the former an orphan boy whom Mankamu had reared. Ipa's baby, Tamaenta, was slung in a strip of barkcloth from her shoulder. Though he was probably two years old, he was placidly sucking the breast which he had located in spite of the unaccustomed clothes.

There was hardly a moment of quiet for the next several days. Hordes of Quichua Indians came to "enjoy the Aucas." The Aucas accepted this with giggling good humor most of the time, gathering in a tight circle to eat their meals, or peeping out through the cracks of the bamboo house where they slept. When the plane came in, Quichuas and Aucas rushed to the airstrip to watch it land—the smooth, unbroken lines of the naked bodies presenting a surprising contrast to the wrinkled, often ragged skirts and blouses, trousers and shirts of the Quichuas. Dayuma soon asked that all the Aucas be provided with clothes, so Dr. Tidmarsh distributed what he had bought for them in Quito.

We introduced them to the wonders of electricity, wood stoves, organ music from a tiny portable, and Diesel motors. They made

"The Lord is my Light and my Salvation; whom shall I fear?" I believed that, and asked Him daily, in the quiet hours before dawn, for light for that day. It was through my Bible reading that He led me to the decision to accept Mintaka and Mankamu's invitation to go to their tribe with them.

few comments on this sort of thing. They were more interested in the meat which I had ordered—forty pounds of beef, twenty pounds of fish, fifty pounds of wild pig. It was all gone in a little more than a week, plus of course huge quantities of manioc and plantain which we bought for them from the Quichuas. Many Quichuas brought them gifts of eggs, bananas, sugar cane, and *chicha*. Some stole from them the small trinkets which Dr. Tidmarsh had given them to take back to the tribe. We were eager to get them back to their own territory, and of course very eager to accompany them, but several days' preparation was necessary and there were delays.

One evening Dayuma gave me her version, in Quichua, of the return visit to her people. I recorded my questions and her answers on tape.

QUESTION: When you left here on Wednesday, where did you spend the night?

ANSWER: At the Oglán River. On Thursday we slept at the Añangu River. On Friday at the foot of a hill we slept. On Saturday at the Lahuano. On Sunday morning in a pouring rain Mankamu went on ahead, because my feet hurt. She went to where their houses were before and found no one. Finally she found Nimunga's house. "Where is my brother, where are my children?" she said. "Way down the river," he told her. So she sent some kids to look for them. Soon Kimu and his wife and my mother arrived. Meantime we thought to ourselves, "Mankamu must have died. Perhaps she has been bitten by a snake." So we prayed to God, "Please don't let anything happen to her." I said, "What will we do if she has not come back by morning?" Mintaka said, "We will go back to Arajuno." "No," I said. "We are going on, even if I have to crawl." I said, "Even if they kill me I am going down and find out how things are." In late afternoon, Mankamu and the others arrived. I began to teach them right away. I said, "Why do you kill? Why do you live like dogs? Don't you know we are all of the same family?" When I spoke thus, two of them cried. Two of the men built us a house and we talked far into the night. My mother brought some fish for us to eat. The next morning I made them chop down trees. I said, "Make a nice big place so the plane can come low. Can't you see that if you leave these trees up the plane is going to bump into them?"

QUESTION: Now do you want to live down there too?

ANSWER: Yes, I told them I would come to stay, but if they got mad at me I would run back to the foreigners. I would like to put my son in school and then go down there to live. But first I will take him to see my mother.

QUESTION: Did Mankamu and Mintaka tell their people that foreigners do not eat people?

ANSWER: Yes, they said, "What in the world did you think they would eat anyone for? They think *you* are the cannibals!" "Okay," they said. "We will believe you now, we won't be afraid."

QUESTION: And were these new girls not afraid to come here?

ANSWER: Of course not. They came shouting with glee. As soon as we got to the Curaray they ran around visiting every house. They talked to the women there, thinking they understood. I came up and the Quichua women said to me, "What are they saying? We don't hear." So I translated and then I told my people, "They don't hear you." But they said, "Oh, yes they do. They hear everything." And they went right on talking.

Later when we went to the house to sleep the Quichuas said we had better set some guards because they might run away in the night. I said, "Why will they run away? They came with me. They will stay with me." Then when a dog barked they said that more Aucas had followed us. "They are coming to kill us." They didn't want to believe me. So I sat down and talked for a long, long time explaining to them that they must not be afraid. "Just go to sleep and don't be afraid," I said. "Okay," they said and they went. I said, "I am not lying. All but two are sick and they are not going to come running up here." They must have caught the sickness from us. I had two bottles of medicine with me. My mother was afraid to take it. She said I was trying to kill her with it. She said, "If Gikari comes, she will show us. We will believe her. We will take the medicine. But you, you are just talking nonsense." So Mankamu told them, "This is the same kind of medicine Gikari gave us. Take it and you will get well." I said to them that their stomachs are probably full of worms. I taught them about worms.

"All right," they said. "From now on, we won't eat anything dirty. We won't let anyone build his house upriver, because then he would dirty the water. Don't use the rivers for a toilet, we'll tell them."

QUESTION: So you said that they killed Jim and the others because Naenkiwi told your people that the foreigners were going to eat them?

ANSWER: Partly that, but he just made up things for nothing.

QUESTION: And how do you suppose they managed to kill them?

ANSWER: The foreigners were just standing in the river and they speared them.

QUESTION: But didn't they fight on the beach?

ANSWER: That is all they told me . . . they just said they speared them. So then I talked to them about the nice foreigners. They said, "Now we understand. Now we see that we did that for nothing. It was only because Naenkiwi and Gimari lied."

QUESTION: Did they watch the burial of the five?

ANSWER: They said they didn't see anything. . . . I told them about the trail to Arajuno and about Dr. Tidmarsh's house. I said if the downriver people come to kill you, you can run there. They said if they had known there were any foreigners there they would have gone to see them long ago.

QUESTION: So they did not understand the gestures from the airplane which tried to tell them where the foreigners lived?

ANSWER: Yes, they understood, and they followed them as far as the Curaray. But they said, "The airplane still goes farther away. It goes way beyond where the hills look blue. We will never be able to reach there." So they turned around and went home. Two men climbed hills and trees, trying to see where it went. "No," they said, "it goes too far away into the blue."

QUESTION: So they have never seen the settlement at Arajuno?

ANSWER: No, it was only Muipa and his crowd who had been there in the time of the Shell Company. And they are all dead now.

QUESTION: Do you think they killed Honorio because he had received Mintaka and Mankamu?

ANSWER: No. That too was because of a lie. Dawa [the third

woman who came with Mintaka and Mankamu and later re-turned] told them that she expected the two women to be eaten. The men who killed him had no idea which one he was. Maruja told me this story. "We were going downriver in a canoe and the dog started to bark. I said to my husband, 'Now we are going to die. It was because you wouldn't listen to me that you brought us down here.' The Aucas threw a spear from the beach and made Honorio fall. I grabbed the fish spear and jumped to the bow of the canoe. But then I said to myself, 'No, I will die with my hus-band.' Then a man named Nimunga caught me in the back of the knee with a spear. The others began to throw rocks at me. So I fell and they caught me. They led me as far as a stream where they washed the blood from my knee, tied it up and then led me on the trail. When I got tired, they took my hands and helped me up the hills. When I couldn't walk, they carried me. When I got to the house, the women heated water and washed my knee. They squeezed *chicha* and gave me some to drink. They baked bananas and gave me some. They gave me roast meat and soup. Then when I came to life a little bit, they said they had better cut my hair like theirs. I did not want them to cut it. So they waited for many days. One day I got sick. They said, 'If we don't cut your hair, you will die.' So I said, 'All right, go ahead.' "

So she came to her home with us when we came out. The clothes she had were rotten so I gave her new ones. Now she is at her mother-in-law's house at the Curaray.

QUESTION: Was her mother-in-law happy to see her?

ANSWER: She didn't know her. She just thought to herself that she was another Auca. Maruja said, "How are you, mother?" Looking at her, the old woman began to cry. "My daughter-in-law!"

The three women, Dayuma, Mintaka, and Mankamu, were agreed that Rachel and I should accompany them back to their village. Valerie would of course go too.

"All that I told you I would say, I said to them," Mankamu told me. "My people said yes."

Delays have always been hard for me to take, particularly when I contemplate a step which I dread. This was one of those. It was

the step to which I had looked forward for three years, and for which the past year had been spent in language study. I had prayed for the privilege which was now mine.

I watched the Quichuas who were my friends. They came into my house as they had always done, talked to me, made themselves at home. I could understand their language. I loved them and did not want to leave them.

I watched Valerie playing with her Quichua friends, eating from a table on which were plates, cups, and silverware. I saw her asleep in the bed Jim had built for her just before he died. I knew that she would not have a bed in Aucaland.

I looked around at the tiny house—it had walls, floors, and furniture. I had even a desk where things were organized. I knew what to expect in an Auca house.

I had a small glimpse of the meaning of the words of Jesus, "What can I say, Father, save me from this hour? No, it was for this very purpose that I came to this hour." He could not ask to escape it. He asked for His Father's will to be done.

He was called the Son of *Man*. As we understand Him we understand life and are enabled to accept it. I could accept this too, if I could be sure of that one thing—that it was God's choice, not merely mine, that I go. In a sense every decision is a matter of life and death—George Macdonald said, "All that is not God is death"—but this one seemed quite obviously so. One evening my Bible reading fell at this passage: "O Lord, Thou art our Father; we are the clay, and Thou our potter; and we are all the work of Thy hand." Somehow this gave me peace. The simple knowledge that I and the Aucas were as helpless in His hands as clay. That we were all His. That, because I could call Him Father, I had nothing to fear.

Rachel was in and out of Arajuno several times during that

Mintaka, Mankamu, and Dayuma went back together to their people and told them that the foreigners were not all cannibals, after all. They responded with an invitation to Rachel and me to come and live with them. Valerie made friends quickly with those who came out to invite us.

week, making her preparations. I began to assemble the things I would need to take. There had been other occasions when I had made jungle trips and thought I had taken the "barest minimum." It had required several Indians to carry. This time, so far as we knew, we would have to carry our own, so the minimum was going to have to be considerably barer than before. I made out a list of things that seemed indispensable:

Bible	toothbrush
notebooks	comb
pen	needles and thread
ink	knives
matches	insect repellent
pot for cooking	calendar
medicines	blanket
one change of clothing	container for Val's milk
shoes	powdered milk
soap	plate, cup, spoon
salt	camera
snake-bite kit	film

I weighed these items. Fifteen pounds. I knew from experience that six pounds feels heavy after a few hours on a jungle trail. I did not see how I could eliminate any of them, and I wanted to take also my tape recorder, language files, a teapot, and other books. They would have to be left until another time. I put some things in a box for the pilot to drop to me by parachute if we found, after arrival, that the dropping of supplies for us would not be objectionable to our hosts. In this box I left more milk for Val, sugar, Nescafé, seeds to plant, writing paper and envelopes, books, language notebooks, and a very few other small items. Even these reminded me of how hopelessly complicated our "civilized" lives have become. The questions of health, comfort, and efficiency had to be weighed again, against the advantages of simplicity and conformity to the Indian way.

We left Arajuno on October 6, 1958—ten Aucas, five Quichua men acting as carriers, Rachel, and I, with Valerie in the same wooden chair carried by Fermin in which she had gone to the Curaray a year earlier.

In midafternoon we arrived at the Quichua settlement on the Curaray River, where we were kindly received and fed. Maruja, who herself had been a captive of the Aucas for nearly a year, we found safe in the home of her mother-in-law. Dayuma and Mankamu had persuaded Mankamu's husband Gikita to release her and had brought her home again.

"In my opinion," she said, when I inquired what she thought of our going in, "it will not be long before you are all dead and eaten by vultures."

"Did you learn to love the Aucas?" I asked.

"The women, yes. Not the men. Not those fierce ones. They are no good." She described for us in detail the treatment of the body of Robert Tremblay, a Canadian who had entered Auca territory just a few months before us, and who, they said, had committed suicide. "He, too, was eaten by vultures. The Aucas laughed. They gave his teeth to the children for playthings."

"I wondered again if I do right to come," I wrote in my diary that night, "and to bring Valerie." But I knew that it is not well to go back on a decision which has been made in the integrity of the heart before God, unless the reasons are *unmistakable*.

The next morning the Quichua men who had promised to take us down the Curaray River as far as the Añangu, where we were to go south, seemed to be questioning their "guidance" too. The canoes were all too leaky, they said. Dayuma had told us we would be on the trail three days. "She's crazy. It will be four or five," they told me. One thing and another delayed our departure, but at last we were in the canoes, traveling northeast on the Curaray. The river was low, and crystal clear, so the Indians poled slowly, watching for fish, alligators, or turtles. By noon they had caught enough to make themselves a large lunch, so we stopped on a sandy beach and they soon had great pots steaming on the fires. It did not take long for the fish to cook, and the eating of it took a matter of three or four minutes. Then we were again on our way. We spent that night in leaf shelters at the juncture of the Añangu and Curaray rivers. Next day we traveled up (south) the Añangu, the Indians spearing fish and stirring the sand as they went, in order to scare up any sting rays. These treacherous creatures lie just under the surface of the sand in the river bed so that they are usually invisible even in the clearest water. When disturbed they stab their victim with a saw-toothed spike, injecting a poison from glands at the base of these saw teeth. Sometimes the flesh of the foot is badly torn when the spike is removed, and the wound takes weeks to heal.

After two or three hours of poling upstream, we left the canoes and traveled on foot for another three hours. I thought of the passage from the psalm which had come to me months before: "Who will bring us into the strong city? Wilt not Thou, O God?" We were very close, now, to what had seemed a "strong city" indeed—an impregnable fastness.

The Aucas who were with us were simply coming home. The Quichuas were approaching those who had been hated enemies as long as they could remember. All six of them had their guns on their shoulders, although Dayuma had assured them that there would be no danger to any who were her friends. Valerie was asleep on the back of Fermin. She knew no fear—she was going to "Mintaka's house," as she had prayed. For Rachel and me it was a moment of high excitement, but the dominant feeling was one of great gratitude.

We came around the last curve of the Tiwaenu River. There stood three naked Indians in front of a small cluster of thatched huts. The "strong city"!

5

The Strong City

THERE IS NO need for faith where there is no consciousness of an element of risk. Faith, to be worthy of the name, must embrace doubt. In our going into Auca territory there were risks aplenty, so far as we knew. There was also the ground of our faith, the Word of Him who is called the "Pioneer and Perfecter of our faith." Nothing less could have brought us to that place. I know that there are many who take similar risks for the sake of adventure or scientific study. I am not one of them. I am afraid the "moment of truth" would elude me altogether if I were to seek it in high adventure. I prefer to seek Him who said, "I am the Truth."

We knew ourselves to be completely in His hands. Not more so at that moment than at any moment in our lives. Neither were we any more doing our duty at that moment than at any other. But circumstances made us more conscious of realities. There were no distractions, no props, no sound of what Samuel Rutherford called "the confused rollings and wheels of second causes."

For me the Aucas were the personification of death. Death is the one thing none of us is willing to face, and the one thing we shall be forced to face. Edna St. Vincent Millay wrote:

This I do, being mad:
Gather baubles about me,
Sit in a circle of toys, and all the time
Death beating the door in.

White jade and an orange pitcher,
  Hindu idol, Chinese god,—
Maybe next year, when I'm richer—
  Carved beads and a lotus pod . . .

And all this time
Death beating the door in.[1]

The door burst when my husband was killed. And the Aucas, these whom we had come to see, had been the dealers of that deathblow. In quite a different way I had been forced to face death, i.e., the Aucas, at the time Honorio had been killed on the Curaray River. It had seemed likely then that death might come to Valerie and me. And now, as Rachel and I went into the little settlement, although neither of us ignored the possibilities, I felt prepared to meet them in a way that I would not have been had I not earlier embraced them and all that they signified for me, by faith.

Psychologists tell us to "do the thing we fear." Good advice, probably, for conquering the smaller fears. It would hardly apply to the great fear, the fear of death. There is only one answer for this—to know Him who holds the keys of death and is Himself the Lord of Life.

Standing on a great balsa log gesticulating and declaiming as we entered the clearing was Kimu, a powerfully built man of about twenty-five. He was naked but for a *kumi*, a skein of

---

[1]"Seige," from *The Harp-Weaver and Other Poems*, Harper & Brothers, New York. Copyright 1923 by Edna St. Vincent Millay, 1951 by Norma Millay Ellis. Used by permission of Norma Millay Ellis.

cotton string around his hips. Great holes in his earlobes were plugged with disks of balsa wood, and his hair was rather irregularly clipped—Dayuma had given most of the men and boys "crew cuts" to help rid them of lice.

Two pretty girls, also naked except for the same string around the hips, stood smiling beside their tiny leaf shelters. Their hair was cut in bangs from the tops of the ears straight across the forehead, hanging to the shoulders in back. I was immediately impressed with the great dignity and simplicity which characterized them. Faced with six Quichua men who were dressed in foreign clothing and carrying heavy loads and shotguns, the Aucas stood quietly and gazed steadily, showing neither fear nor self-consciousness. One of the girls Dayuma introduced to us as Gimari, her sister, whom we recognized as "Delilah" in the photographs taken by the five men on "Palm Beach." She carried a beautiful baby boy in a sling of barkcloth over her shoulder. The other girl, slimmer and graceful in every movement, was Dawa, Kimu's wife.

Mankamu went over to the man and thumped him on the shoulder. "Gikari!" she called to me. "This is my brother! This is my own brother!" He was still declaiming. I had not the least idea what he was talking about, and was too occupied in trying to talk to the two girls to make any attempt to write down his speech. Soon he seated himself on the log, Mankamu at his side, talking continually. Valerie sat down too, and fixed her eyes on him, the first Auca man she had ever seen. I had told her plainly that her father had died, that he was living now "in Jesus' house," but I had said very little to her about how it had happened. I had wanted to save it until she could comprehend it more fully. Somehow, however, her mind had associated Aucas with her father. I watched her study Kimu's face. Finally she spoke.

"He looks like a daddy. Is that *my* daddy?"

So these who had spelled "death" to me were to Valerie human beings, her own. She identified herself with them and was ready to accept as her own father the man who had helped to kill her father. There was nothing strange to her about the Aucas. She had been reared in an Indian environment. These were simply Indians, her friends. She had prayed that the Lord would "take us to Mintaka's house." Here we were, and she was content.

When the first excitement of arrival was over, the women who had come with us quickly set to work preparing a meal of fish that had been caught on our way in. The Quichua men were invited to eat, and they all squatted around the leaf spread on the ground, Kimu among them, as though two months ago they would not have killed each other on sight.

As twilight fell, we all gathered on the logs lying about the clearing, and the Quichuas sang some of their simple hymns, much to the amusement of the Aucas. Quite voluntarily Fermin broke out in prayer, nothing of which was understood by the Aucas.

"Our much beloved Father, you have brought us safely to this place. Here we are with our new friends. We say thank you very much. We love them, we prayed much for them. Show us how to live together like brothers. Open their hearts, plant your Word in them like seeds which will grow."

We were very grateful as we lay down on the bamboo to sleep that night. Once more we had seen the Word of God worth trusting. He cannot prove this to us unless we act upon it.

Before dawn I was awakened by Kimu going past my hut. "I'm going. Gikari! I'm going." He was on his way to notify the others of our arrival. They were living in another location. Dayuma had chosen the one where we were, close to where she had lived as a child, and asked that the entire community join us. In order to be close to their sources of food, the majority had stayed at home until they heard that we were there. Late in the afternoon of that

Val was a little baffled, but not frightened, at her first view of an Auca man. "He looks like a daddy," she said of this one. "Is that my daddy?"

Dayuma had made clothes for nearly everyone in the entire group, but some wore them only when they were in the mood. For this picture—the largest group we were able to get together at any one time during that first year—Dayuma saw to it that those with clothing occupied the front row.

second day, and for several days after, the Aucas arrived, family by family or in twos and threes. There were fifty-six in all, a few of whom did not show up for several weeks.

Seven of these were adult men, the oldest being Gikita, a man of perhaps forty-five. He was lucky to have reached this age. The odds against a man were great in a tribe where spearing was so common. Each of these men had a family and of course there were a number of widows. The rest were fatherless children. Not a very impressive group, considering how they had held their neighbors in terror for centuries and captured the interest of the world during the last three years. There was one other group of Aucas, the "downriver people," who lived perhaps a hundred miles away and were the most feared enemies of "our" group. Ten of their number were now living with these, included in the fifty-six we had counted. They told us that the downriver people were more numerous, probably numbering between a hundred and a hundred and fifty. There were no more, so far as anyone knew, except for two who lived isolated somewhere near the Napo River.

The few single women in the group were beautifully formed. The mothers seemed unusually ravaged by childbearing. The men were all muscularly built, some stocky, some lean and wiry. The children were very healthy-looking for the most part, with none of the symptoms so common among other jungle people— the distended belly, scrawny neck and limbs, which betray intestinal parasites.

Except for the crew-cut males, all had heavy black hair cut in the same bangs from ear to ear, hanging shoulder-length in the back on the men, longer than that on the women.

When they arrived they made no particular sign of recognition either of their friends or of us. They usually took a seat on a log and began to talk, eying us rather casually from time to time. One

Dayuma's aunt, Gami, and mother, Akawu. They have long ago removed, as a sign of mourning for close relatives, the large balsawood earplugs which filled the perforations in their earlobes.

or two fingered Valerie's yellow hair, asked if she were male or female. She was not, so far as I could tell, an object of any special interest to them. They were not, as so many have supposed, "captivated" by the little blonde foreigner.

It was hard for me not to make some move toward them, to "greet" them in some way, or to touch them. I saw, however, that this was not done. I was a foreigner, and more conscious of it than I had ever been in my life. I was, for the first time, among a people who had had no experience whatever with foreigners. To them I was not an American, not a "knowing one," as some of the Quichuas called us; certainly I was not a member of the benefactor race. Apparently the testimony of Mintaka, Mankamu, and Dayuma had been sufficient to convince the Aucas that we were not malefactors either, but I doubt that there were many points in our favor.

I tried to imagine what it must mean to them to find us there. Most of them had never seen anyone whom they did not know. And here, in a familiar place, they came upon strangers; a strange color, strange sizes, speaking a strange language; a people whom they had always believed to be cannibals. And these people, according to the three women, would live here now and be their friends! What were their true feelings? Can they possibly have trusted us?

Yet, in a matter-of-fact way, they accepted us. Not with open arms, to be sure. It is not their custom to receive anyone in that way, even their own children. But neither was it with malice.

And so we had come—to these who have been called one of the

I experimented with a few words in the Auca language on "Delilah" and Dawa. They seemed baffled—perhaps by my American accent.

Gikita took a special interest in seeing that I understood the language. Often he would imitate my mistaken pronunciation of an Auca word and then repeat it correctly time after time. "Do you hear?" he would say. "Gikari, do you hear? Do you hear?"

most savage tribes on earth. We were in their homes. We were outsiders, however, and we had come to show them the Way. What right had we to tell them that we knew a better way than theirs, to assume that anything we had to offer could possibly be meaningful to them, let alone wanted by them? We knew that we must earn that right. We must live with them, love them, try to understand them, and above all, demonstrate to them what we meant by eternal life: a new *kind* of life, not simply a longer one. We had not come to show the Auca ways of improving or prolonging his temporal life. Even what we call the benefits of civilization were unknown to him and seemed to us of more and more dubious value as we learned to know him better. We had come to offer something which, apparently, the Auca was not even looking for: a Hope, an anchor for the soul, the person of Jesus Christ. We were witnesses of Him. As Paul said long ago to the Corinthians: "We can enlighten men only because we can give them knowledge of the glory of God, as we see it in the face of Jesus Christ."

6

A Place to Hang Your Hammock

Our new home was a clearing about seventy-five yards in diameter, bordered on the west and south by tall forest trees and on the north and east by a curve of the Tiwaenu River, a clear-running stream normally twelve or fifteen feet wide. When we arrived there were half a dozen very small huts in the clearing and two precarious-looking "houses"—mere roofs of woven palm, supported by six palm poles about twenty feet high. The Aucas had been warned that I was tall. I am not sure whether they thought I was that tall! Later they added second floors under these roofs, which helped the ungainly appearance somewhat. Rachel was invited to share one of these houses with Gikita, his wife Mankamu, and her children (his other wife, Umaenkiri, had a small house close by), and I was given a smaller house adjoining theirs. None of the houses was anything more than a roof. The total absence of walls, even though the houses were either joined together or within a few feet of one another, seemed to bother no one but me. I would have been glad, now and then, to be able to

go into a room and close a door. Valerie did not seem to notice the lack of walls, floors, or furniture. She had her "bed," two or three bamboo poles, split and flattened and laid across three logs on the bare ground. On this she soon spread out her doll's blanket, a little scrap of cloth, and was immediately at home.

The Quichua men made two small tables for Rachel and me, constructed of four sticks stuck into the ground with bamboo laid across the top. It was a great help to have something on which to put things—there was literally nothing else except the bare ground where we could prepare a meal or mix Valerie's milk. We could not sit at these tables, since there was nothing resembling a chair.

We hung our belongings in duffel bags, baskets, and Indian carrying nets from the ridgepole of the house. (I could easily reach the highest part of my roof, and could not stand up at the sides of the house.) When it rained, it rained in. Often the tropical rains came so suddenly that things got wet before I could put them away. If I happened to be working on the language, which was most of the time, I had to put away my files, my notebooks, my papers and three-by-fives in plastic bags or hang them high enough under the roof so that they were out of reach of the rain. I had a radio, two cameras, a tape recorder, and any number of books or papers which had to be kept dry, to say nothing of our clothing and ourselves. Here was where I began sincerely to envy the Indian. He had nothing which would be harmed by getting wet except his blowgun, which was always stored up underneath the thatch. Even that was covered with a kind of pitch in case he should be caught out hunting in the rain. But he did make an effort to keep it dry. Other possessions included a dart case, which was waterproof, a hammock, which he sometimes tied in a knot high off the ground to raise it above the splash of the rain, several clay pots and fishnets, a knife, some baskets, some gourds for drinking, his spears, which were also stored in the thatch, and a few trinkets of little worth to him which he had collected from airplane drops. As for himself, he did not mind in the least getting a little damp. He simply squatted by the fire and sat it out. He did not have to rush around closing windows, and, until they began to adopt some of the "advantages" of civilization, his wife did not need to think about getting the clothes off the line.

Man always adapts himself to his environment, but to see the way another man has done it, in an environment which seems anything but hospitable to human habitation, is always impressive to an outsider. At first glance, one might ask of the Auca way of life, "Is this the best they can do?" but one soon finds that "this" is very well indeed.

In the first place, Aucas are semi-nomadic. They do not want to settle permanently in any one location, mainly because they seldom use a plot of ground for planting more than two or three crops, and also because they are never sure when their enemies may make it advisable to move. And perhaps they just enjoy a change of scenery.

So their houses do not require a great deal of time or effort to build. One man can build a house for his family in two days. I even saw a woman build one by herself in a few hours—a small one, of course. They know which palm will resist insects and jungle rot. These are used for the main standards of a house which is to last more than a few months. They dig a posthole with a machete, lift the post, which, if it is ironwood, is extremely heavy, and drop it as forcefully as they can into the hole. They repeat this several times until the post is firm, then pack the earth tightly around it. Grooves have been cut in the tops of the posts, in which is laid the ridgepole, usually of bamboo. The rafters are made of a lightweight but very strong reed, the *caña brava* of the Amazon region, which has the advantage of being not only strong but almost perfectly straight. Across these are laid the roof leaves. There is one palm whose leaf may be used for temporary housing without weaving. It seems the Lord created these palms especially for use on roofs—each leaf is the length, or at least half the length, of an average Auca house and needs only to be split down the center and tied across the rafters. If the roof must last for five years or so, the raffia palm is used. The leaves are split in the same way, and each frond is woven. These are laid three or four deep and tied with jungle vines; they provide not only a watertight covering for the house but also an excellent insulation against heat and the thundering noise of tropical rain, which in this area falls at the rate of 120 inches annually. The smoke from the fire inside the house coats the leaves with tars which act as a preservative from insects.

The Aucas learned about matches years ago when they stole them from Quichuas or received them in airdrops from the Shell Oil Company. But they seldom need to use a match. The fire is kept burning continually in each house. It is needed in the day-time for cooking and for some slight protection from insects, and at night for protection from animals as well as for warmth. For contrary to popular belief, not all jungles are hot and steaming. This area is in the western extreme of the huge Amazon basin, nearly in the foothills of the Andes, where there is an elevation of about fifteen hundred feet. The climate is ideal, with warm, often sunny days and cool nights, a mean temperature of seventy-two degrees. It is said that in diversity of forms and profusion of indi-viduals the flora produced here is the richest in the world.

Although we found it necessary to use clothing, blanket, and fire in order to keep warm at night, the naked Auca is comfortable so long as his feet are warm. His fire is right beside his hammock, and he sleeps with his feet in the smoke. When the fire dies down enough to cool them off, he wakes and simply reaches down, without having to get out of bed, and pushes the logs closer together. Occasionally he sits up and rubs his hands over the flame to warm them. In the morning, a woman need only reach for a pot of food, usually cooked the night before, and set it on the fire. Breakfast is ready before she gets up!

The only furnishing in an Auca house besides the fire is the hammock. This is the most versatile piece of furniture ever de-vised. Woven of a lightweight, strong palm fiber, it is portable, takes no floor space whatever, and is extremely comfortable for either sleeping or sitting. If one sits with the feet on the ground

OVERLEAF: *A hammock had not seemed to me very com-fortable until I learned to lie in it as the Aucas do, diagon-ally. Then I found it marvelously comfortable for sleeping, eating, studying. The fire was within reach of the other side, so that I could cook as I worked on the language, and keep warm as I slept.*

the hammock serves as a stool or chair. When the feet are propped up it becomes a contour chair. When it is spread out it makes a very comfortable bed in which one sleeps diagonally on an almost horizontal plane.

It did not take us long to recognize the superiority of this method over our own. The airplane dropped me a hammock identical to the Aucas', though made by a different tribe. I learned to keep my fire going, too, and it was very cheering to wake on a windy, rainy night and find it glowing warm beside me. Valerie slept on her bamboo slab next to my hammock, in a blanket which I had folded and sewed up two sides, forming a bag. I had found it impossible to keep her covered if she slept in a hammock, and on the bamboo there was no way of tucking the blanket around her, so I devised this method, which proved satisfactory.

The hammock was a "kitchen stool" on which to sit while I cooked, and an ideal place in which to study. I could use Valerie's "bed" for a table on which to spread my language materials, and relax as I worked. I sat in it while I ate, and I lay in it in the evenings and read by candlelight. Often I shared it with Valerie while we read a story, or with an Auca who wanted to talk. It was expandable, and quite comfortable even for two. Auca husbands and wives usually sleep in a single hammock, and often a parent and child will share one.

There is much to be said for and against "identification," the attempt of a foreigner to live as do the people among whom he works. It has been tried in varying degrees and ways in many parts of the world.[1] I have tried it myself in some measure. I should like to remind the reader again that I lived with the Aucas less than a year.[2] It may be possible to do certain things for a limited period which could not be done over an extended period, although it seems to me that our adaptation to Auca life would have been workable indefinitely. I have been able to come to no conclusions about the effectiveness of identification, from the standpoint of the Indians. Whether or not my efforts to

---

[1] See Daniel Johnson Fleming, *Living as Comrades*, Agricultural Missions, Inc., New York, 1950

[2] See epilogue.

identify led them to love me, they most certainly led me to love them. "It is by loving, and not by being loved, that we come closest to another person."[3]

We had no choice in the way we lived. We were given an Auca house; we lived in it. It was no dream house. Besides the total lack of privacy and cleanliness, there was the lack of protection from rain, insects, and even snakes. I began to contemplate making some improvements one night after finding a snake coiled near Valerie's head as she slept. There was no way of doing this, however, without introducing new problems which we wanted to avoid at that time.

The most trying factor of all was the insects. It is easy to say that Indians are used to the bugs, that they are immune, that a for-eigner's health would be impaired if he did not protect himself. I do not believe this is true. Indians suffer from insects. They are not immune, though it appears that some degree of immunity from toxic effects may be developed. I have never suffered any permanent ill effects from the bites of insects. When I have com-plained about what a nuisance they are, the Indian has agreed heartily, though he does not as a rule complain about them him-self. They are a part of his life, and he has learned to accept them as he accepts all the things which we call hardships. He does not pity himself because of them. In the worst of the gnat season the Aucas seem almost to acquire a rhythm in their constant move-ment to swat the pests. They slap their backs, brush their legs, move from one foot to the other. On hot days the sweat bees de-scend in hordes, crawling into nose and mouth, ears and eyes, swarming over the food, often lighting by the dozen on a mouth-ful as it is being passed from pot to mouth. These creatures will not be shooed away. They must be picked off one by one.

A dear lady whom I do not know sent me a gift of money ear-marked for screens for my Auca house. To what does one tack screens when there are no walls? It is often said that a missionary ought to show the people a better way, a "higher" standard of living. But screens, at least so far, would be an impossibility for the Auca. Have we a right to use them ourselves, and thus add one more barrier to the high ones which we cannot eliminate? I do

[3]George Macdonald.

not know. Jesus Christ, when He was here on earth, lived on a lower standard than most of His associates. He had not "where to lay His head."

There was nothing about Jesus' customs or everyday life which was peculiar. He followed the customs of His time and country. He was the expression of His Father, come in the flesh and living among men. There were no distractions to His message in the way He conducted Himself among them. To them He was not a foreigner. "Let Christ be your example as to what your attitude should be. For He, who had always been God by nature, did not cling to His prerogatives as God's Equal, but stripped Himself of all privilege by consenting to be a slave by nature and being born as mortal man" (Philippians 2:5—7, Phillips' translation).

I began to comprehend, while living with the Aucas, something of what it means to be a foreigner, to lose one's own culture for the sake of winning those of another. I began to appreciate, as I had not appreciated in six previous years of missionary life, the necessity for removing as many of the distractions from our message as possible. Was I bringing them a foreigner's message, or had I something to offer which would mean Life to them, the very Life of All Ages, as John refers to Christ in his first epistle? If He is the Life of All Ages, He is the Life of All Cultures.

7

Menu: Manioc, Monkey, and Nescafé

ONE OF THE first questions asked about any people is, What do they eat? The Aucas haven't much variety in their foods, but they have plenty of nutrition and, according to one doctor to whom I described their diet, a good balance. There is no problem of undernourishment. They are, in fact, an exceptionally robust tribe. I found no diseases among them except one or two uncertain cases of malaria, which is endemic among their neighbors the Quichuas, and the common cold. One woman died, after the entrance of Dayuma, Mintaka, and Mankamu, from what sounded like pneumonia. Perhaps a new strain of bacteria had been brought in, to which they had no resistance. There were none of the "children's diseases" of civilization: mumps, measles, chicken pox, whooping cough, scarlet fever. Parasites, the curse of the tropics, apparently did not infest them in sufficient numbers to cause more than the mildest symptoms—an occasional case of diarrhea, or stomach-ache. I treated some infected sores, but the Indians had a remarkable resistance to these and seemed to recover equally well without treatment of any kind. There were several people in the group who displayed deep scars from spear wounds. They described to me how they had been pierced. (One old woman had had a spear through her ribs which passed clear through from chest to back.) They had either yanked out the spears, tearing the flesh seriously on the sharp barbs, or left them in until the wounds rotted and maggots ate a hole big enough to enable them to remove the spears. The scars in each case were as neat as a surgical incision.

Only one or two babies were born during our stay in Tiwaenu (the name of the river on which we settled)—both successfully— so I have no way of knowing what the infant mortality rate is.

The fresh air, sunshine, hard exercise, and long sleep must account for some of this ruggedness. The diet undoubtedly plays an important part. The most primitive men lived solely by hunting, fishing, and gathering. The Aucas have advanced one notch above this—they do these things, but they also practice simple agriculture. Their staples are manioc, or cassava, the starchy tuber which thrives in Amazonia, and the plantain. They clear a new section of the forest nearly every year, discarding and burning the underbrush and leaving the largest tree trunks lying wherever they fall. Using a stick, they make holes in the ground, into which they insert manioc or plantain starts. A minimum amount of weeding is all the care necessary for these, and in five months they have a crop of manioc, plantains in a year. Manioc is to the jungle Indian what potatoes and bread are to us. He rarely eats meat or fish without great chunks of boiled manioc. The women prepare a food-drink by boiling and mashing the manioc, then chewing and spitting a small portion of the mass to start fermentation. Mixed with water, this is drunk on the second day, a stringy, lumpy liquid of a milky consistency, which seems to be very nourishing.

The men spend the greater part of nearly every day hunting. The task would be big enough in a community where the proportion of men to women was fairly equal, but where the number of men has been decreased sharply through the years by spearing, the men have all they can do to support their own wives, their sisters, in-laws, and any other widows who happen to be living with them or next door. They start out at dawn, having eaten a large breakfast of meat, fish, manioc, and plantain drink. Usually they announce what it is they intend to hunt that day—howler monkeys, woolly spider monkeys, squirrels, toucans, or macaws. For these they carry a blowgun, a long flattened tube of heavy palmwood with which they shoot poisoned darts.

The poison is presumably curare, though I have never been able to verify this. It is prepared from the bark of a jungle vine, which is scraped with a sharp knife, packed into a leaf-funnel, and moistened. The funnel is secured between sticks and the juice is allowed to drip slowly into a small clay pot. After several hours the liquid is simmered very gently over the fire, great care being taken not to let it boil. The Indian watches it closely, and as skin forms on the top of the chocolaty syrup he lifts it delicately with the tip of a dart, wipes it on a shard of pottery, and, as it cools and thickens, gives each dart a deft twist in this paste, then props the dart neatly in a tiny rack made of two darts stuck upright in the ashes near the fire. When they are dry the poison looks like a dark coat of shellac and will keep its potency for many months. They are stored in a case made of a hollowed stem of bamboo, fitted with a waterproof lid of bark and pitch, and equipped with a set of piranha teeth, from the deadly fish said to attack wounded animals or men. (None of the Indians I have asked has known of any such case in Ecuador.) The piranha inhabits the streams of the eastern jungle and is sought for its excellent meat and sharp teeth, which are used to make a tiny groove around the tip of a dart. When the dart strikes a monkey, he will often attempt to pull it out before its paralyzing action has taken effect. The groove causes the dart to break, leaving the poisoned end in his body.

The dart case also has a gourd of kapok tied to it. The Indian picks a wad of this and with a single twist forms a little plunger on his dart which serves to carry it through the blowgun.

One day I was invited to go on a wild-hog hunt. Kimu had been chopping trees. Suddenly he came racing into the clearing, shouting, "A herd of hogs!" He grabbed his two spears, gulped some *chicha*, whipped off the bathing trunks he was wearing, and headed for the forest, followed by Naenu, Dawa, and me.

We soon left the trail (or at least the last vestiges of what I call a trail) and plunged up hills and down, across streams, under logs and vines, through mud and thickets of thorns. Each time we came to a stream there would be the trail of hog footprints in the sand. Of course the Indians had been following these all along, but I never saw a trace of them in the underbrush. How they did it—and at top speed—is still a mystery to me. It was not long before I was hopelessly confused as to direction, making it all the more imperative to keep close behind the Indians because I could not have found my way home alone.

Presently Gimari and Ipa slipped by me like two naked sprites. I had thought they were staying at home, but somehow they had caught up with us.

I lost track of time, but I suppose an hour had passed when the single file of Indians, led by Kimu, stopped abruptly and spoke in the lightest of whispers, "Here they come!" I was incredulous. Why would the pigs do a right-about-face and come back along the very trail we were following? Somehow Kimu knew that this is what they would do, and I could hear them now for the first time, though he had been following their sound. They seemed to be a big herd, grunting and rushing toward us. I had my camera ready but wondered what I'd do when that wild pack bore down upon us. Gimari whispered, "Stand still beside their trail—like this. They won't stop to bite you. They will just tear past. You take pictures!" Everyone stood statue-still, Kimu with his powerful right arm raised high with the red-dyed, feathered spear poised horizontally, every nerve tense. The rush and roar seemed to be within thirty feet. The animals sensed us. They turned at right angles and fled, their sound completely dissipating in a second or two. I began to believe the stories I had read of how large animals can move noiselessly through heavy jungle without

A wooly spider monkey or gatan *is the children's favorite playmate. He once ate my entire week's supply of fresh beef while I was attending one of Dayuma's Sunday meetings. He thoughtfully replaced the meat with a washcloth in the soup.*

shaking so much as a leaf. Everything was as still as before. A bird screeched far away, and Kimu disappeared after the hogs. The women decided to go home, so I followed, disappointed to have been the only one who did not see the hogs.

Kimu returned three or four hours later laden with a good big sow. He went out again next day, followed the same herd (he knew where they would spend the night), and came back at nightfall with a boar and a piglet. The latter he had captured with his hands and intended to give his wife for a pet, but it bit him so he ran it through with a spear.

Sometimes, when the rivers are running clear, the crowd may decide to have a fishing expedition. Occasionally they take with them a poison root which, when dumped into the river, stuns the fish so that they are easily caught by hand. Usually, however, the men sharpen up their long supple fish spears and the women take their scoop nets, beautifully woven of palm fiber and strung on a wooden hoop.

The men go first, sometimes sending a boy to dive and see if there are fish in the chosen pool. If not, they move to the next. Often a school of fish flashes by and with shouts and laughter they chase it. A lunge—"*Baru!*"—the spear is whipped high out of the water, the fish slides down the shaft, spins brightly as the Indian cracks its head with the knife he holds in his left hand. He flings it in a gleaming arc to the beach where it is picked up by one of the women and roasted immediately in the fire she has made or is put into one of the palm-leaf holders the women make to carry home. All this happens in a matter of seconds, while the rest are racing after the other fish, missing them half the time, miraculously impaling them the other half.

The women work along the edges of the rivers with their scoop nets, pushing them up under the trailing vines and leaves which line the banks, trapping small fry. Valerie loved to accompany them on fishing trips, for she had learned to slide along the river bed on her hands, watching closely for the tiny armored catfish, cupping her hands quickly to seize them as they clung to the underside of the rocks. These she carried home in her own little leaf package, suspended from a strip of bark around her head.

Arriving home again late in the afternoon the women set to work immediately building up the fire which has smoldered all day. They clean the fish, usually leaving the scales on, and always leaving head and tail intact. They fill the largest pot with manioc and fish, set it on the fire, and then prepare to smoke the rest of the fish, as this is the best method of preservation. They have never known salt in any form. They collect green sticks about an inch in diameter and build a platform over the fire, placing the cleaned fish on it and covering them with green leaves in order to concentrate the smoke.

When the boiled fish is ready each mother serves her own family group—her husband, if she has one, and her own children, plus any orphans for whom she is responsible. Dabu, who has three wives, eats with each one, in her own section of the house where she has her private fire.

The quantities of manioc and meat which an Auca can eat at a sitting amazed us, but we ought to have taken into account the fact that they had nothing else. No appetizer, no salad, no bread and butter, no beverage, no dessert. What we eat in variety and quality, the Auca makes up for in quantity. And then he has the ability to go for long periods without anything at all to eat. Rarely does an adult get a noon meal. Children who are at home most of the day nibble at an ear of corn, a few peanuts, or a morsel of dried fish. But the hunter takes nothing with him but his weapons, and the woman takes no food with her to the manioc patch when she goes out to work.

They know how to get all the good out of a food, too. Monkeys are singed whole and cooked with the skin on, so that the thin layer of fat which lies under the skin is not lost. The tail is smoked and eaten; heads are eaten with brains, eyes, ears, and all. Sometimes even the teeth are carefully pulled and thoroughly sucked before being thrown away.

The sole diet of a certain squirrel is a species of palm nut. So the stomach of that squirrel is a great delicacy. It is roasted in the ashes and eaten whole, with its contents.

Meat and fish are not the only protein foods. Indians relish the great pale grubs which are the larvae of a giant beetle. These feed on palm heart, and the Indian knows the telltale hole they make on entering. He cuts down the tree and digs them out, bringing them home squirming and heaving in a leaf package, to be eaten raw or roasted in ashes. These provide fat as well as protein.

Even bones are not thrown away until they have been cracked open with a knife handle and the marrow has been sucked out.

No utensils are necessary except the cooking pot, which is either an aluminum one, received in the "gift-drops" which the five men initiated, or as a gift from one of us, or a clay one, made by the Auca women from clay got in nearby streams. There is no dishwashing problem. The food is lifted from the pots with the fingers, thrown onto plantain leaves spread out on the ground, and grabbed by eager hands. There is a great slurping and sucking for the few minutes that the meal lasts, but that is all—the idea of conversing during mealtime is unheard of. There is one job at hand, and everyone throws himself into it with zeal and concentration. He would get little to eat if he didn't.

When the evening meal is over, it is bedtime. This, too, is a simple process. No need to get undressed, no beds to prepare, no teeth to brush—for though the Auca does not clean his teeth, they are nearly perfect, unless he is one of the old ones. The lack of any sweets in the diet may have something to do with this.

When we first entered the tribe, Rachel and I had hoped to live almost entirely on the Indian food. We had been told that Indians have a balanced diet—carbohydrates, proteins, vitamins—and we saw for ourselves how healthy they seemed to be. Quite apart from the obvious advantages of not having to import food, we hoped that this measure of conformity to their way of life would hold its own advantages. Here, again, our Master had left us an example. He ate what was given Him, in the company of ordinary men. He was not aloof from their feasts, their dinner parties, their simplest suppers. He even cooked for them—a breakfast of fish and bread, served by a charcoal fire on the lake shore.

We had taken some basic foodstuffs with us, not knowing what the sources of supply might be. I always kept powdered milk for Valerie. But when we were invited to share Indian food, we accepted it gratefully. Valerie had lived all her life in the forests and nearly always preferred jungle foods to foreign ones.

I had not fully anticipated, however, the difficulties which would be involved, first of all because of the lack of a medium of exchange. While living in Quichua territory, it was a simple thing to ask for food—eggs, plantains, manioc—and pay for it in currency. The Aucas had no use for money or anything else which might have served as a trade item. We found ourselves in a difficult position. Either we waited until we were given food, which was frequently but not regularly, or we asked for it. The women told me several times to ask for food, and sometimes I did, but it was not an easy thing to do. I realized that I had nothing to offer them, and women were expected to cultivate their own staples. Then there were times when there was nothing for which to ask. I could see that the Indians' supply was gone, and, although they were accustomed to go without food and make up for it with a huge meal later, we were hungry.

At last it became evident that we must have a separate source of supply. We had hoped to be able to do without scheduled food drops from the Missionary Aviation Fellowship but found we had to request them. Consequently, every Friday they flew over, dropping mail and meat free-fall, and other items such as powdered milk, Nescafé, sugar, oatmeal, cheese, and bread by parachute.

It was an exciting time for all of us when the "beetle" (the Aucas' name for the airplane) buzzed toward the clearing. Any who were in nearby garden patches or at the river came running at the shouts of *"Ibu, ibu!"* Kumi, a teen-age boy, started up his "announcing" of the plane's circling. Women shrieked at their children to get clear of the place where the stuff would fall. Some of the timid ones headed for cover. Either Rachel or I manned the radio, to find out how many drops to expect and learn any news the pilot might have for us. Several wide circles and treetop-level swoops were necessary to drop the week's supplies. The boys

OVERLEAF: *"Be it ever so humble . . ."* Val was happy at home with a potful of manioc and meat to eat and a bamboo bed to play and sleep on.

and younger women rushed to recover the bundles when the signal was given "That's all!" Then the Indians crowded into our houses to inspect the haul. Dairy products such as milk, cheese, or butter were sniffed and occasionally sampled. The reaction was nearly always one of disgust. "It *stinks*! Are you going to *eat* that?"

I usually gave one of the men the job of cutting up the hunks of frozen beef. "It burns!" they said of the coldness. Each family was given a piece, however small it had to be. We wanted to share with them whatever we had that they liked. They had shared their food with us. Some of the younger boys liked almost anything they tasted. They waited for candy, sugar, or oranges, if there were any, while the older ones disdained sweets of any kind.

The mail had to be opened in their presence, too. They learned to recognize the brown envelopes in which magazines arrived, and grabbed them before I had a chance, laughing over the pictures, joking about those which resembled someone they knew. And the letters had to be read and the contents summarized before some of them were satisfied.

"Is that all, Gikari? Did you look at all?"

"That is all."

"She says that's all. Let's go."

The obtaining of food was not the only problem. Cooking it presented others. We had, of course, no stove. Our cooking arrangements were the same as the Aucas'—a fire on the ground.

The getting of firewood was a problem for several reasons. It was my desire to be one with the people wherever possible. There were enough things that I could not do. This was one that I felt I could do, although with difficulty, of course. I am no woodsman. I found, in Tiwaenu, that it takes a strong arm to swing the big axes which the Aucas have (obtained from air-drops and from Quichua homes which they have raided). I found, too, that it takes a sharp aim to split wood. I could cut it fairly well, but when it came to splitting I provided the Aucas with a hilarious comedy. They nearly always offered to do it for me and were sometimes told to by Dayuma, but I knew that the other women were expected to get their own wood, and I did not want to set myself apart from them by not taking this responsibility. I do not know, however, whether this idea had any useful result other than giving me some good exercise and teaching me a useful skill. I think the Aucas rather accepted it as another of the foreigner's amusing whims.

And then, when the meal was cooked and eaten, we had to wash dishes. This was not a difficult process, but it seemed so absurd—the ritual of soap and sponge, pot, spoon, bowls and cup, the plastic container in which I shook Valerie's milk. All this paraphernalia had to be carried down the muddy bank to the river. And *three* times a day. "There she goes again," they would say. "She's going down to wash her pots and her plates and her clothes [for often I combined these operations] and her daughter."

I was hopelessly a foreigner and felt pretty sheepish about it.

8

The Best Things
in Life Are Free

SAVAGES, BEING HUMAN, love to play as well as civilized people. Here in Tiwaenu there were no books, no movies, no television, no sports, no organized games of any kind, no hobbies, no clubs, not even a fiesta during the entire time I spent with the Aucas. There was monotony—same scenes, same few people, same routine day after day. There was no mental stimulus as we think of it. There was limited space in the clearing. The houses were huddled close together, the hammocks strung in a crowded tangle in some houses. Conversation was limited to what seemed to me a very few subjects: food, the hunt, past killings, sex. In short, I would have thought they had all the ingredients for neurosis. This was not the case. They found plenty to do.

First of all, they work. This takes a great deal more time than I had supposed it would. We say that people in tropical areas are indolent. I do not think this term describes the Aucas.

I recorded carefully what Mankamu did one day. At four-thirty

I woke to hear a soft cracking sound. She was sitting up in her hammock, peeling manioc without the use of any implement save her hands. She would tap a stick of manioc all around with another stick, split the skin and peel it off with her fingers. Another sharp tap on the top of the stick split it into long pieces, which she threw into a pot. Then she blew up the fire and set on her pot. After breakfast she packed up a basket of plantains, manioc, peanuts, and sweet potatoes which must have weighed seventy pounds. I tried to lift it and couldn't. She stooped down with her back to it, pulled the strip of bark up over her head, and heaved herself and the basket up. I accompanied her on the trail. She walked more slowly than she would have done without the basket, but her pace was steady, up hill or down, through rivers and over rocks. Ipa was with us too. She had as big a basket as Mankamu, plus her two-year-old child swinging from her shoulder in a piece of barkcloth and a package of *chicha* in her hand. At one point she slipped and fell, managing to land in a sitting position so that the baby was unhurt. The load jerked her neck backwards as it fell, and she squashed the package of *chicha*, but she hopped up cheerfully, picked herself a new leaf to make the package again, set the carrying-band on her head once more, and started off without a word, or even a "Whew!"

When we reached our destination, probably twelve or more miles away, Mankamu set down her load, cooked a big meal, swept the house, chopped wood, walked a mile or so downriver to get a jungle pod for eating, chopped a staircase into the cliff going down to the river, set up a platform over the fire, and spent the whole night smoking fish.

I felt shamed for ever having pitied myself, or for having thought of the Indians as lazy.

When not at work, the Aucas thought of many ways to divert themselves. The smallest happening in the clearing was the subject of conversation. If two roosters (which they received in a gift-drop from the plane) had a fight, everyone watched with the greatest glee. If someone stumbled carrying a pot of water, the attention of everyone was called. If my pot fell off the three logs which supported it, dumping the contents into the fire, the community rocked with laughter. "Gikari's pot fell!" It was shouted from one house to another. "Gikari's pot fell!" "All of it?" "All of it! Ha-ha!"

Birds which flew across the clearing they watched as Americans watch cars or planes, identifying the species as we identify makes and describing their flight in excited speeches like a sports announcer.

"Ah! Two macaws! Husband and wife. Here they come. There they go, there they go, there they go. Right toward the kapok tree. Into the kapok tree—no, they're going around. Ah—two more. They are all together now. Where will they land? I'll shoot them, all four of them—*watik, watik, watik, watik*—with my darts."

Everyone enjoyed teasing animals or children. Dogs, which the Aucas had never owned until Dayuma took three puppies in, were a new diversion. They pulled their tails, petted them, fed them till they were the fattest jungle dogs I had seen. The boys teased them into frenzies of barking by shouting and waving palm fronds at them. Monkeys were well fed and fondled, and often cruelly treated. It was not uncommon to see a human baby sharing his mother's breast with a pet monkey. Children were laughed at if they fell or hurt themselves, just as adults were. Sometimes the adults amused themselves by lying to the children to hear them scream. "Your mother has gone for good. You will never see her again," a child was told, wakened in the middle of the night when his mother went outdoors for a moment. Or, when Kimu was building a bonfire to burn off brush, "Kimu is going to roast you. You will burn so that we may all laugh."

Valerie took her share of this, too. She came shrieking to me one day, having been told that Dabu was going to chop her up with an ax. The same man who said this would, at another moment, patiently show her how to roast a green banana in the coals of the fire.

"The dark places of the earth are full of the habitations of

OVERLEAF: *Never underestimate the power of a woman. Bai, dubious at first about the idea of clothes, prances tentatively, submits at last.*

cruelty." It is true. Cruelty in any form, anywhere, is not to be excused. But because their forms of cruelty were different from ours were they therefore *worse* than ours? We have often observed the cruelty of children in their treatment of each other. This is as true in modern America as it is in primitive Tiwaenu. A handicapped child is the brunt of his playmates' jokes; a child who hurts himself is laughed at; the shy or lonely child is shunned by the rest and made shyer and lonelier. When we reach adulthood, we condemn this behavior. We are subject to certain pressures which modify our conduct. How often is it social consciousness rather than conscience that is responsible for this modification?

We practice instead other forms of cruelty. What is cruelty but indifference to the suffering of others or the desire to inflict pain? From what else springs the integration "problem" in the United States? What is the root of the spirit of rivalry and faction, the delight we know in undercutting an enemy, excelling our neighbor, or shrugging off another's misfortune with "Serves him right!"

We are horrified at lies told to children. Yet we not only condone but are amused at anything—no matter what it may have cost someone else—which is called "only kidding."

We have confused inhibition with virtue, refinement with righteousness, propriety with purity.

If the Auca is indifferent to the sufferings of others (and perhaps he is not so indifferent as he appears to us) he is indifferent to his own. He can laugh when he hurts himself. He does not pity himself. To be free from self-pity is to be well on the way to adulthood.

Play, as Auca boys know it, usually means practicing spearing. The men teach them, using all sizes of spears—from tiny ones the size of a broom straw, with which spiders are impaled, to the nine-foot palmwood lances with which wild pigs, anacondas, alligators, or people are killed. The boys often toss a banana stalk into the swift-running current of the river and chase after it with their fish spears, vying with one another for the best aim. Each thrust of a spear is accompanied by sound effects: *"Baru!"* ("There!") or *"Ba-ah!"* ("Take that!").

The children know how to snare large bumblebees with a thin strand of palm fiber without getting stung. These they "fly" as American boys fly toy airplanes, and the bumblebee has a real live, buzzing motor which never needs rewinding. When they get tired of this, they tie a tiny wad of cotton or kapok on the other end of the string and watch the bee sail off into the forest, trailing the white speck in the sunlight.

They go out at night and spear large hoptoads without killing them, then place red coals on the creatures' backs and watch the glowing "taillights" bounce through the dark.

They are not always sadistic. They shoot tiny birds with blowguns, often pluck their feathers before killing them, and roast them to eat. But if the bird seems to have survived the dart especially well, they will most tenderly nurse him back to health with tidbits of food, spending hours hunting for crickets to feed him, cradling him gently in their hands, and setting up a tiny perch for him with a leaf roof, where he can feel at home.

There is always the river, an endless source of diversion. Everyone bathes and plays, the adults sometimes swimming with the children on their backs so that only the child is seen above water. The boys, like boys in any old swimming hole, shout and dive, duck one another, race, shriek false alarms which might well be true: "Anaconda!" or "Electric eel!"

Conversation, of course, is the commonest form of entertainment. Most of them love to talk, and there are several real champions among them, who can hold forth for two hours or more without a break, and without more than an occasional grunt from a listener for encouragement. Early morning is often the social hour. Someone wakes, stirs up his fire anywhere from three to five in the morning. He decides it is near dawn, wants a little companionship, and starts talking. If he gets no response, he wakes someone purposely to listen to what he has to say. I have been wakened on numerous occasions and been told that the

OVERLEAF: *Dabu and Valerie have in common the ability to amuse themselves with simple pastimes on a lazy Auca afternoon.*

moon was shining, that Munga was a liar, or simply that someone was on his way to urinate.

Once the conversation gets rolling, everyone may join in, no
matter whether he is in the same house or not. What one says is
relayed to the farther houses by the houses in between, and so it
goes, round and round, several shouting at once, Rachel and I
frantically trying to get at least something from one of the speak-
ers, or put something down on paper. Rachel declares there's
nothing like a few hours of language study before breakfast to
fix it in your mind!

Often the day began with someone singing. I got used to this
and would sleep through it for a while, hearing in my dreams the
far-off, nasal twang of the male voice. It sounded to me like a
jew's-harp. There is a method of using the vocal chords which I
cannot imitate—always very nasal, often horn-like, beginning
and ending with an explosive catch in the voice, and sustained
through hundreds of repetitions of the same series of notes.
There are two, or at most three, notes in each "tune," and the
words change perhaps every ten to seventy repetitions. Subjects
ranged from narratives, made up more or less on the spur of the
moment, through lyrics about orioles, flowers, rivers, to a word-
less nasal chant of two tones, sung in the dark by one of the
women. Whether this was equivalent to "whistling in the dark"
to keep up courage, or perhaps a substitute for the juke-box
mania of America, which calls for *noise* in the background, I
did not know. There could be far more subtle reasons, or perhaps
the Aucas simply like to sing.

There are, so they tell me, occasions when they dance. They
demonstrated how they do this. Long lines of women spread out
side by side across the clearing and simply walked backwards
and forwards, singing. Or the men and women placed hands on
one another's shoulders, in a long line, and jumped, coming
down with both feet flat on the ground at once, chanting as they
went.

As women in America amuse themselves in a practical way by
knitting or crocheting, Auca women spend nearly all their time
when they are in the houses, apart from cooking, in rolling the
string to make hammocks or fishnets. It takes them nearly a year

to make enough string for a hammock. The fiber is a palm leaf similar to the famous *paja toquilla*, used in the making of Panama hats. It must be gathered at a certain stage of development, the leaves stripped down in a certain way, and the strands boiled and sun-dried, then rolled on the bare thigh with the palm of the hand. This makes an extremely strong and durable twine, of any desired thickness, from the finest sewing thread to package twine.

Then, of course, an entirely new diversion was to watch the foreigners. There was hardly a moment of the day or evening when at least some of the children were not watching us, asking questions, sorting through our belongings.

Pulling out a package of dried soup mix, or a fountain pen, they would ask, "What is this?" Usually I knew no Auca word to describe it. Then, "Who made this?" Now it made no sense to say to an Auca that you did not know who made a thing which you owned.

"Did your husband make it?"

No.

"Did your father make it?"

No.

"Did you make it?"

No. In fact, I had to tell them, I had never seen the one who made it. Incredulous stares.

"Then why did he give it to you?"

I knew no way to explain to them trade and currency.

Turning to something else, "Do you know how to make these?"

No. Then they turn to something simpler, which anyone should know how to make—a clay cooking pot.

"Do you know how to make these?"

No.

"Do you weave hammocks?"

No.

"Do you make fishnets?"

No.

"Do you plant manioc?"

No. Then, in despair, "What *do* you do?"

"Well" (desperately trying to think of something) "we write. We make marks on this paper." The look said, "What a useless way to spend one's time!"

The Aucas wanted to try it, too, however, and it did not take them long to learn to look at pictures and recognize things even if they were upside down. They spent endless hours thumbing through my *National Geographic* magazines. When one boy had been through an issue, questioning me, he then showed it to another, reciting all the answers I had given him. They in turn would repeat the comments, sometimes in unison, to a third.

They tried out all my pens, ruining three good ones for me. They collected all my discarded letters, smoothed them out, carried them around, used them to practice writing on, showed them to their friends. When the mail came, they hung over my shoulder.

"Who wrote this? Does he live far away? Have you seen him?" They learned the names of all my brothers, my sister, my parents, and many of my friends, hilariously trying to pronounce them and calling each other by those names.

Valerie had many children's books sent to her, with pictures of animals dressed in clothes. This fascinated them. It was enough of an anomaly to see human beings in clothing, but when rabbits and squirrels wore them— They went back again and again to the picture of a weasel dressed in trousers, carrying a shotgun. The children soon learned that this was "just a drawing, for nothing," but it was hard to convince some of the adults that the foreigners' animals did not have guns.

Valerie was a great help in entertaining my many guests. She showed them picture books, shared her crayons and coloring books with them. The teen-agers, and even the adults, enjoyed coloring. People occasionally sent this sort of thing from the United States, along with a great many other toys which, after the first moments of excitement, were relegated to a dilapidated

The mind of the savage may be an open one, a very honest one. The simplicity of these two was a bond of communication I sometimes envied.

basket where the crickets made short work of them. Valerie had brought with her to the tribe, however, one single toy—a doll. This was a marvel to the Aucas. It was something they could comprehend. They pulled off its arms, legs, and head (it was plastic and easily reassembled) and laughed themselves nearly sick.

Valerie's favorite toys, however, would have horrified her grandmothers: a large hunting knife and a fire. The knife was rather dull, and she spent much time hacking away at old stumps or at the poles which supported my house, cleaning weeds as the Auca women did with their machetes, or digging holes. She learned to use the knife quite skillfully and was able to help me peel manioc and plantains.

She loved to build fires. She learned to build them even in the rain. When she played "house" with the Auca children—an entirely new idea to them—she of course had to have a fire for them to squat around. She found endless diversion searching for small twigs or chips from the trees the men had chopped down. Then she would take a burning stick from someone's fire, as the Aucas usually did, and soon have a nice little blaze.

For me, there was seldom any problem of babysitting, or of trying to think of ways to amuse my daughter. I sometimes wished I could think of ways to keep her at home a bit more. Occasionally she did not come home even for lunch, she was so occupied with the joys of the jungle and her Indian playmates. One day I kept a record, for the benefit of those who felt so sorry for the "poor little girl with no toys and no white playmates," to see just how she spent her time:

She spent the morning bathing, fishing, cleaning weeds, cutting papaya stalks to make toy blowguns, helping the girls roll logs off the airstrip [Dayuma had encouraged her people to start work on this], tending her can of tadpoles. This afternoon she is upriver in the canoe with Kimu, and the little boys, watching them spear fish. After lunch she went with Iniwa [a boy of about ten] to dig sweet potatoes on the beach. Then he took her to the plantain patch where he cut the blossoms from some of the trees. There is a drop of nectar at the base of each which the children love to suck. . . . Thankful today that Valerie has a wealth of things which matter far more than a clean bed, a dry house, shoes, starched dresses, or visits to museums. She has the love of God, the river running by her bed at night and the stars shining where she can see them as she lies down; she has the joy of misty dawns in the forest, of night birds and crickets and monkeys; of brown naked children who are simple and unaffected; of little pets—tiny green birds, yellow birds, brown birds, diminutive monkeys, all tamed by the Aucas who seem to know and understand their ways and are forever patient and unforgetful in caring for them.

9

The Civil Savages

THE AUCAS, BEING so few in number, are a close-knit group. Probably everyone is related in some way, though their moral code forbids them to marry first cousins. There is no formal social organization, no government, no central authority of any kind. Community activities are almost unknown, except for the rare "feast" where everyone joins—I do not know for what occasion—to share a big drink. They drink the common food-drink *chicha*, which among Quichuas is fermented more highly for a feast but among the Aucas is drunk in its mildest stage of fermentation. Intoxication is unknown.

There have been many rumors circulated about Auca chiefs—very fierce ones, tall ones, red, hairy ones, fat ones. The Aucas tell us they have never had a chief. Every man is his own boss. The only social unit is the family, and even the head of the house is hardly recognized as such. Each of the adult men now has only one wife, with the exception of Dabu, who has three. One of Giki-ta's two wives died shortly after we arrived. A husband may tell his wife to do something, but she seems to get away with disobedience. Dayuma says the men never beat their wives, seldom even get angry with them. I never saw the slightest sign of friction between husband and wife. I saw Dabu, when he had been bitten by a snake and was still very weak, tell his three wives to help him get roof leaf—he had been bitten when his house was only half-finished, and the rain was beating in on him as he lay in his hammock. The wives said *"Bah!"* (*"No"*) and that was that. Dabu went and got it himself.

Gikita was building a large house, requiring many heavy palm poles and tons of roof leaf. He had a strapping teen-age son, Kumi, who I noticed spent most of his time teasing and chasing younger boys, or simply sitting in the house. I asked Gikita why Kumi didn't share the work with him. "I told him to, but he said '*Bah!'* " was the reply. I never saw one man help another in any task unless it was something that would benefit both. If two men planned to live in the same house, then of course both men worked on it.

Women, likewise, were responsible for their own families and had no community projects equivalent to the quilting party, where the work of all would benefit only one. They of course went together on fishing trips, and caught their own fish, but when they returned, each usually shared her catch with some of those who had not gone.

Dabu's three wives were responsible for feeding their own children, and Dabu took a share of what each prepared. He slept most of the time with only the most recently acquired wife. From all appearances the three got along beautifully. I often marveled at their congeniality. They would sit in their hammocks, each in her own corner of the house with her children's hammocks hung around her fire, and call back and forth to one another, sharing the day's gossip and events. There had been moments, we were told, when the oldest of the three, the only witch doctor in the Auca community, showed her jealousy of the youngest of the wives. She would get up at night and go over and blow up the fire where Dabu and Wiba slept, and shake the hammock to waken them. Neither Dabu nor Wiba did anything about this intrusion.

There seems to be no marriage ceremony as such. No marriages occurred while I was there, but those I heard about differed. One took place at a dance. It was the consensus that Wiba would make a good wife for Dabu. Dabu already had two wives, and enough children to keep him working hard. He was not eager for a new wife. But in the midst of the dance, someone took Dabu's hand, another took Wiba's, joining them and making them dance. This was "a wedding."

On another occasion, a young man came to the edge of a clearing, beckoned to the maiden he had chosen, and she followed him into the forest. This was not an "accepted" method, but it worked. The girl's stepmother rushed after them in a rage, knocked their heads together, and said, "What do you two think you're doing?" But they were considered man and wife from then on.

Sometimes the man went to the girl's family and asked for her hand. This was what Naenkiwi had done. Gimari's brothers, however, refused. Naenkiwi had at least one wife already. Gimari should be given to another. But Naenkiwi insisted, threatened her family, and finally made a clandestine affair of it. Not long afterwards he was killed by his own brother-in-law and another. This may have been an example of tribal discipline: the death penalty for stealing a wife. Or it may have been the obvious means of self-protection, since Naenkiwi had threatened the lives of the other men. It may have been both.

Discipline is not very highly developed in the family. Children are sometimes whipped with nettles when they disobey, or flogged with jungle vines. It was my impression that punishment as such was very rare, and that parents tended to wink at disobedience unless the issue was an important one, which affected the adults' comfort, such as a child's crying with temper in the night so that everyone is kept awake. Sometimes when the men returned from the hunt all the children were lined up and whipped hard, one

OVERLEAF: *A married couple at home. For the most part, Auca men are faithful to the wife or wives they have chosen. Occasionally, by mutual consent, brothers trade wives, or sisters trade husbands, for a limited time.*

after another. This, they said, would make them good hunters. After a day clearing jungle or working in the manioc patches the adults would often slap the children with nettles from head to toe, including their faces and eyes, "to make them hard workers."

The older women had a right to order the younger, but they were not always obeyed. I saw younger women refuse with impunity. If the older made enough fuss about it, however, the younger usually complied, for, like other Indians I knew, they preferred to avoid making an issue if public opinion would be against them. As soon as the rest of the community noticed any contention, they joined in with enthusiasm, and the underdog became the object of united scorn. When this happened the loser accepted the taunts and jibes with surprising grace. I noticed the same thing when one of the women who especially liked to give orders was loudly criticizing the way another was doing something. I would have been strongly tempted, had I been the other, to tell her to mind her own business. The Auca woman quietly went on with what she was doing, simply ignoring the jeers, or asked, "Is this the way you mean?" and took the advice. I found myself the object of this sort of criticism many times, even when I was doing something about which the Indian had not the remotest idea—loading a camera, arranging a radio aerial. On one occasion four of us—Gimari, Kimu, and his wife Dawa and I were untangling several hundred feet of rope. It seemed a hopeless task, and none of us was sure of the best way to go about it. Dawa appeared to be, however. She gave the orders—in a loud, raucous voice, reminiscent of the proverbial fishwife. "Let go! No! Do it this way! Bring that end here. Oh, look at how that bonehead is tangling it all up again. Leave it alone. Let me do it. Hold still! Hold this. What do you think you're *doing?*" It was very wearying, but her husband took it quite calmly, both he and Gimari ignoring the directions and doing it the way they pleased. It was one of the occasions when my tongue was bridled only by force, not by virtue. I could not say what I would have liked to say.

Public, rather than private, criticism seemed to be the rule. Only rarely did I hear an Auca criticize another behind his back.

Munga was a man from the enemy group, the "downriver group," and was tolerantly but not very cordially received. Now and then I heard jokes made about him, and unfavorable criticism. For all I know, however, the same things may have been said to his face. Malicious gossip, the bane of Small Town, U.S.A., was a rare thing among the savages.

In fact, many of our civilized sins were conspicuous by their absence. I noticed almost no vanity or personal pride, no covetousness, avarice, or stinginess. The men were not lazy or selfish with the spoils of their hunting—when a man brought back an animal, it was divided among his own family, his sisters if they had no other man to look after them, any widows who needed some meat, and Rachel and me. The Apostle Paul had to write specifically to the Corinthian church to rebuke them for not caring properly for their widows. The Auca does this without knowing any law but his own conscience.

Any guest who comes to an Auca house is given a place to sleep and food to eat. Not immediately, perhaps. I arrived at one house after a half-day's journey, having had nothing but a baked plantain for breakfast. Mankamu was with me, and I knew that she had had nothing more. When we got to her brother's house, we were not greeted. There is no greeting in the language. They saw us coming downriver and stood on the bank and watched. Then they went back into the house, and when we arrived no one spoke. We walked in, and stood. There were several hammocks empty, but no one said, "Sit down." I was tired, and probably Mankamu was too. She began to talk, as only she can do, on and on and on, telling the details of our journey and the health of her own family. Finally, without an invitation, she sat down. I followed suit. I was desperately hungry and thirsty. There was food in sight, but Mankamu said nothing about it. After two hours we were offered a half-gourd of plantain drink—ripe plantains, boiled and squeezed by hand into a paste and mixed with water. My thirst made the first bowl go down easily. The second was not so easy—the mixture is full of lumps and strings, lukewarm in temperature, and of a somewhat rotten flavor. My heart sank when I saw the third bowl—each bowl is about quart capacity—being prepared. I could probably have refused it without offending them. There is no ritual connected with this drink, nor any special significance that I know of. But it is nourishing, and I was aware that there was likely to be nothing else offered, so I took it.

Later, other members of the family arrived. They had not known we were coming, but they showed no surprise, and did not speak to us. I have seen Aucas arrive, after weeks away from their families, and say nothing to any of them by way of greeting or recognition. They simply take up the conversation as if there had been no separation at all.

"Oh, they're just like animals. They don't know what love is." This is not true. It is perfectly true that they ordinarily express themselves very *differently* from the way we do. But it has been said, "There is no feeling in a human heart which exists in that heart alone—which is not, in some form or degree, in every heart."

Valerie was, as I have said, an object of no special interest or affection among the Aucas. I saw little evidence of any special fondness even for their own children. There was one occasion when a mother, in describing a snake bite from which her son had already recovered, wept loudly. But that same mother thought it a great joke when her little son was showered with sparks as she fanned the fire. He cried out in pain, only to have his older brother fan more sparks on him, which the mother thought even funnier.

Mankamu wept several times in speaking of the little daughter who had died. Mintaka told me that when she saw the dead child in its father's arms, and the father crying over it, "it made us cry."

Mintaka was also one of those who laughed as they told us the story of Umaenkiri's death. She had become delirious and rushed out to the forest, crying that the spirits were calling her to come. They followed her, chased her back to the house, and she fell dead into the fire, burning her hair as she fell. Mintaka, who was her sister-in-law, and Watu, who was her niece, laughed at the memory.

I once asked Gimari and Ipa, the two widows of Naenkiwi, if they thought about, loved, remembered (there is only one Auca word) their husband. They giggled. Perhaps they were embarrassed by the question and did not want to reveal their true feelings.

Perhaps they were expressing them accurately. Then they asked me the same question: Did I think about, love, remember my husband? "Yes," I said, "very often." They laughed at this, and asked why anyone would remember one who was dead.

One evening Kimu told a long tale about the death of one of the Auca men. His introduction included extremely meticulous details about several narrow escapes from death which the man had had before he was finally killed by a spear. One of these was a snake bite. As Kimu described the effects of the bite, the pain, delirium, and struggle to get home assisted only by his wife, he laughed. "Oh, it was something! He fell over every root. He bumped into trees. He cried, he groaned and moaned, 'Let me die. Here I am going to die in the forest. Leave me at the foot of this tree.' But his wife pulled him by the hand, in the dark. Ha-ha! She really had a time of it. If she had not been there he would surely have died all by himself. Ha-ha! But she got him home, just at dawn. He lived after all."

Tales of the endless killings which have taken place are told with the greatest animation. The narrator remembers who speared whom, and in what part of the body. Often revenge is taken in exactly the same way, the killer specifying the reason for each blow as he plunges the spear: "*Baah!* You speared my father's hands. Take that and that. *Baa! Baah!* You speared his chest—*baa*—on the right side and—*baa*—on the left. You speared his stomach, his head, his legs. *Baah, baah, baah!* Take that, and that, and that!"

This is the code of law. It is not a new one—an eye for an eye. If I asked why they kill the "downriver" Aucas, the reply was always the same: "They kill us."

One day Dabu pointed in a northeasterly direction as we were sitting on the sand by the Curaray River. "Over there is the trail of the downriver people."

"When will we go to visit them?" I asked.

"Visit them? Visit *them?* Gikari! You don't want to visit them!"

"Why not?"

"Why, they're *killers* down there!"

"And are you not killers too? You kill people, don't you?"

"Oh, Gikari! We just *kill* them. *Those* people, when they kill, they cut off their legs. They would cut off your legs, too, if they killed you. They would pull out your eyes. They would chop you up in pieces. They are killers."

And I realized again that the "savage" is not insensate. He, too, is shocked by certain types of behavior. He has his ideas of what constitutes murder. The Scripture clearly tells us that the man who *hates* his brother is a murderer. That man is always a murderer. The man who kills may not always be one.

As I write this, a leading news magazine comments on the week's events: the success of an American president in his efforts to balance the nation's budget; the interest of the free world in aiding underprivileged nations; a campus sex orgy involving eleven students of a respected eastern university; the arrest of a professor for the alleged murder of the dean of a graduate school; the indictment of a borough president for criminal conspiracy to obstruct justice; the premeditated bombing of two airplanes. The editorial comment: "It was a week of excitement, a week of scandal and human tragedy, yet a week with a certain meaning: despite man's highest aspirations and achievements, the human clay is still far from porcelain."[1]

Human clay is not closer to porcelain in certain places, certain cultures, certain ages, than in others. What do we mean when we speak of one people as being more "needy" than another? What do we mean by "savage"?

Man has one desperate need. It is God. This means redemption from self. Christ came into the world to offer this redemption. One man, by his own efforts, or by whatever we may call progress, is not in any wise capable of making himself *less* needy of Christ than another man. I realized that I had thought of the Auca as being particularly needy, unconsciously equating the level of his culture with the level of his morals. Now I found "raw" savagery no more awesome than the familiar variety. I thought of the words of Jesus: "This *is* the judgment—that light has entered the world and men have preferred darkness to light because their deeds are evil."

This judgment is wholly impartial. It is without reference to

---

[1] *Time*, January 25, 1960.

social organization. The Auca apparently knows no such organization. He knows nothing of drunkenness or wife beating. He may kill his neighbor, but he does not fight with him. He may not participate in any community projects, but he shares his one small monkey with the widow next door. He may practice polygamy, but he faithfully supports all of the wives he has. He does not greet a friend or bid him good-by, but he entertains without charge any guest who happens in, even if he is a Quichua Indian whom he has never seen. He does not wear clothing, but he has a strict code of modesty and is totally free from the American preoccupation with the human body, and all the absurd inhibitions this involves. In short, I was faced with the fact that socially I had nothing whatever to offer the Aucas. Any comparison between myself and them, from this standpoint, was painful to me. Why was I here?

There was no answer but the simplest, most elemental: Jesus Christ. To obey Him, to present Him.

10

The Earless Foreigners

IN EVERY PHASE of life with the Auca Indians I was painfully conscious of my ignorance. I have been asked if I thought the Auca's intelligence was below average. My answer is no. If an Auca were asked the same question about me, I feel sure his answer would be yes. I was ignorant of the Aucas' crafts, of their foods (what was edible, what was not; how to obtain, plant, or prepare the foods), of their customs and legends, of the flora and fauna of their forest, of their history and the long, detailed stories of killings which they knew so well. I even found I could not follow a jungle trail without help. To an Auca the streets of New York would probably look very much alike, though he would not lose his orientation. To me, however, the trails of the forest looked hopelessly alike, when I could see them at all, and often they seemed to disappear altogether and I would go rushing off on what I took to be the trail, only to be called back with "Where in the world do you think *you're* going?" It was unbelievable to the Indian that a white woman could be so heedless.

But nowhere did I sense the gulf between us as I did in my ignorance of the language. This is the area in which, except in the rarest cases, a man remains a foreigner all his life.

Even in America, where our education is supposed to have produced some degree of understanding and tolerance toward all peoples, it is difficult for any of us not to regard one who speaks broken English as slightly ignorant. To say that my Auca was "broken" would be a euphemism. What must they have thought of the two foreign women who jabbered unintelligibly to each other? When spoken to I could offer only monosyllables in reply, often so far from the correct form as to be quite unrecognizable. It was easy to think, "Oh, well, I only forgot to nasalize one vowel. They ought to be able to recognize that." Suppose a foreigner who was learning English said pigpen instead of Big Ben, excusing himself with, "Oh, well, I only forgot to voice one consonant." The difference is not greater between the *p* and *b* to an English ear than between an ordinary *a* and a nasalized *a* to an Auca ear.

One of the greatest difficulties for us was the assumption of most of the Aucas, like Mankamu, that we understood them perfectly. The fact that we got a word here and there, and every now and then managed to produce a whole sentence which was intelligible to them, only confirmed their suspicion that we really knew what they were saying. When on occasions it became unmistakably evident to them that we did not understand, they gave up in disgust and called us "earless," or used a word meaning "their ears are hole-less." They thought for a while that my difficulty was due to the fact that my hair covered my ears. "Why don't you shave the hair in front of your ears so you can hear?" This was too high a price to pay, but I did oblige them by pushing my hair behind my ears for a week or so to prove to them that this did not help.

Several of the men seemed to make a special effort to help me to understand. I was unspeakably grateful for this. Gikita would repeat the name of an animal or flower dozens of times for me. Even after I was quite sure I had reproduced it correctly, he kept shouting it at me, laughing, and asking if I had written it down. "Now you will remember!" he would say.

Dabu would punctuate his conversations with "Do you hear, understand?" (The word is the same.) Honesty frequently forced me to say no. This discouraged him and he would give up the attempt, when I wanted badly to hear him continue, and to try to get what I could. After this I tried to nod ambiguously or repeat the verb he had used in his question: "I hear!" It was the only way to encourage conversation and this was, of course, the only way to learn the language. There is no substitute for hearing it, hour after hour, day in and day out. Some of it is bound to be absorbed at least subconsciously if not through the effort of intellect.

Rachel and I spent nearly the whole of our time in language study. But this could mean anything which we did in the company of the Aucas, as well as actual paper work or informant work. To fish or swim with them, go to the forest to collect fruit, or share their *chicha* around the fire was to study the language. We were never without our little notebooks and pens, listening, straining to catch new suffixes, new uses of words we knew, new intonations, as well as new words.

Intonation is one of the most essential elements of a language. We know that an English sentence can assume any number of different meanings, expressing different emotions, according to the intonation used. The simple inquiry "Where have you been?" becomes an accusation when the first and third words are slurred and heavily accented. In a foreign language it is as important to use the intonation pattern of that language as it is to use the vowel pattern. I had many times been misunderstood when speaking a foreign language and observed others misunderstood, merely because of a mistake in intonation. I have even seen an Ecuadorian turn away in disgust, thinking an American was speaking English to him because the American was using a purely English intonation with Spanish words.

The Auca language, like any other, has its peculiar pattern. There was one habit the significance of which still has me baffled. Certain words—any words, provided they occurred in a given position—were "roared" instead of spoken, with a strong explosive breath which emptied the lungs. Others were pronounced with a sucking in of the breath. This, too, depended on the context or emphasis given to those words at certain times, rather than to an integral element of the pronunciation of the particular word. Often words were truncated to the extent that they were unrecognizable to us. We are inclined to be annoyed by these peculiarities when we encounter them in a language we are trying to learn, but we would do well to sympathize with those who are trying to learn English and who hear Americans use phrases like "Jeetchet?" (meaning "Did you eat yet?"). The old American classic "Jeet?" "No, jew?" "No. Squeet." is not worse than many of the Auca contractions, and of course where there is no written language with which to compare what we record the difficulties are increased.

Verb roots were often employed without the identifying suffixes which tell us who does the acting. There were sounds we could not identify as either vowels or consonants. There were others which were pronounced differently by different individuals. We wrote in the standard phonetic script but have been unable as yet to discover which elements are significant to the language. In other words, there is still no such thing as an "Auca alphabet." Auca can be written, as any human vocal sound may be written, with phonetic symbols. But this is a very different thing from knowing which of these symbols are *necessary* to the language we are dealing with.

One of the greatest helps to the collection of data was my tiny tape recorder, a six-pound machine which ran on four flashlight batteries. It was easy to record conversations, monologues, singing. It was quite another thing to transcribe the material to paper. With the help of Dayuma, who was a very superior informant after long experience with Rachel, I was able to transcribe the material of fifteen *minutes'* worth of tape recording in five hours. This did not include any *translation* of the conversation. Translation, even if we worked through the Quichua language, which Dayuma knew, took another two hours or so, and then any number of hours might be spent in filing the data thus gained. One of the salient features of the Auca language is the use of suffixes. This meant that every word might be filed under five or six different headings, depending on the number of suffixes it contained besides the root. It was by means of this filing, laborious as it was, that we were able to analyze and classify. Rachel and I shared our material, she having already given me, a year earlier, much on which to build. By working independently, however, on separate files, we were often able to supplement each other's work.

Valerie was another help in the learning of the language. It took her almost no time to learn the phrases she needed to get along with the children, and she was soon mimicking the expressions of disdain which are so common, used freely by the Aucas on one another, and just as freely on us. Valerie used them on me. An Indian woman was spinning cotton thread on a very primitive spindle. "Here," she said, handing it to me, "you try it." I clumsily tried. Val walked in at that moment and shouted out the Auca phrase meaning "Everybody get a load of *this!*"

Several times she came to me and said, "Mama, why do you say so-and-so [using my pronunciation of an Auca word]?" "What do the Aucas say?" I asked. She then gave me the correct form. She was very particular about pronunciation of nasals, and when I carelessly omitted them in the use of an Auca name when I was speaking English she mimicked the slip in a loud sneering tone, exactly as the Aucas do, finishing with their expression roughly equivalent to "Listen at her!" It was not that she was disrespectful to me in English. It was simply that she not only spoke Auca but thought in Auca. She accompanied her speech with Auca gestures as well, when appropriate.

Some have asked me if the Auca language is a "rich" one. Here again, as in the question of the Auca intelligence quotient, the answer is relative. It is said that there is no such thing as an "inadequate" language—that is, inadequate for its own culture pattern. The Auca language is extremely rich in onomatopoeia (words derived from the sounds which they represent). I have found it quite impossible to translate fully an Indian man's description of the hunt. His narrative is heavily punctuated with imitation, which are actual words, describing the leaping of a monkey from bough to bough, the chattering of that monkey, the sound of the dart as it strikes him, the plunge from the tree bough, the impact of the body on the ground, the whack of the machete as it finishes him off. There are many words not properly called onomatopoeia which describe ideas associated with some overt action (ideophones, perhaps).

But in the attempt to express abstracts one feels that the Auca language is indeed inadequate. So far as I know, there are no words meaning "to be able," or "to know." Often the Aucas came around while I was speaking on the short-wave radio to Shell Mera. They always asked, "What did they say?" More often than not, if the transmitter said anything more than "O.K." I could not translate it into Auca. I don't know how to say, "I can't translate it," or even, "I don't know." I could only look blank and risk giving the impression that I was withholding information. Or, if they asked, "Is the airplane coming today?" I couldn't say, "I don't know." I could say, "I don't see," which was obvious, since they didn't see it either, or, "I don't hear," which made less sense, since even they could *hear* the voice coming over the radio. They could not understand it, of course, but the word is the same. I once heard Dayuma say, "Coming it will come, not coming it will not come"—apparently her way of saying that she did not know whether or not the plane would come, but it illustrated the fact that literal translations are rarely meaningful, that thought patterns are completely distinct.

And if communication proves so difficult in the material realm, how are we to convey anything of the spiritual? What communication can there be between two such vastly differing cultures? What has one to say to the other? How can it be said?

We know, of course, that the adequacy of the medium does not guarantee satisfactory results of the message. Jesus Christ Himself, the "Personal Expression" of God, "came into His own creation and His own people would not accept Him." He said to Nicodemus, who had questioned Him about the new birth, "If I have spoken to you about things which happen to you on this earth and you will not believe Me, what chance is there that you will believe Me if I tell you about what happens in Heaven?"

But He was faithful in the telling. He expressed adequately and completely the person of His Father, and those who accepted His witness were given power to become sons of God. God put His own Word into man's language. We have been given that Word. We have believed it; we are responsible to see that it is faithfully communicated, visibly and verbally.

Dayuma of course has perfect command of the Auca language. She also has learned a great deal from Rachel which she can teach her people, and she faithfully does so. She wanted her people to have a "meeting" on Sunday morning. First she had to explain to them the seven-day cycle which we call a week, and inform them when the first day came around. At dawn she would call out, "Everyone come. I am going to speak about God." Sometimes it happened that the men had already left for the day's hunting, or the women had gone to their manioc patches, but those who were there usually co-operated with this new idea. They came to the house Dayuma designated, sat down meekly where she told them to sit, and listened with reasonable attention at least for the first few minutes. Dayuma has a wonderful memory for detail, and she would choose one of the Bible stories, from the Old Testament or the Life of Christ, which Rachel had taught her, and tell it to the Indians with appropriate sound effects, gestures, and explanatory footnotes wherever necessary. Her talk was punctuated with admonitions to shut up—for after all, an Auca speaks when he has something to say, and is not accustomed to being told that he must sit in one place and listen to one person for a full half-hour without interjecting his own comments where he chooses.

When it came time to pray, those who had observed the activity before supplemented Dayuma's instructions to close their eyes with "Now we will all sleep. Everyone sleep!" And they obediently closed their eyes, checking now and then to make sure others were conforming. Seeing that Dayuma put her hand over her face, some copied this. All were silent through the long,

OVERLEAF: *"Tomorrow is the day I am going to speak about God," Dayuma said to the Aucas on Saturday. They had no idea of weeks, nor any names for days. Sunday mornings they would gather together while Dayuma spoke to them, simple stories from the Bible, with appropriate illustrations from her own experience and theirs, punctuated rather frequently with admonitions to "shut up," since it was a new idea to them to have to be still while one person spoke.*

long prayer, covering all of Dayuma's friends from the United States to Tiwaenu, with earnest petitions that her own people would think about God, live in a new way, and learn to love their enemies.

Even in prayer, the simplest form of speech, it is difficult to convey in the Auca language the idea of petition. There is no difference between the verb forms in the petition "Will you (please do such-and-such)" and the command "You will (do such-and-such)." The request "May we" is the same as the future declarative "We will." Thus prayer often becomes a recital of all the good things we are going to do, rather than a plea that God will help us to do those things. The Aucas may say to God, "You do well, and we will do thus and so," implying that our action depends upon God's, and so long as the Aucas understand this they have some basis for faith, but I often wondered whether they were bragging or praying.

Sometimes Dayuma would ask them to repeat what she said in prayer. Some were happy to oblige. This may have been a sign of the new birth, but I had to remind myself not to regard as a "spiritual awakening" what may have been the sociable desire to please; nor, on the other hand, to regard lightly the hunger that is in every man, recognized or not. God knows the heart, and He knows which man loves what he has seen of Him. It is not nearly so important that a man learn the forms of prayer as it is that he pray, conscious of his own need of prayer. Until he asks, as a child does of its father, for things of which he knows a need, his prayer is hypocritical. The Auca has, so far as I know, no form of religion. He knows nothing of prayer, sacrifice, worship, placating evil spirits (though he believes in their existence), or adoring the good. He is not consciously seeking after anything.

But obviously the lack of recognition of a need does not prove its absence. We are responsible to present Christ to those who are aware of the emptiness of life and to those who are perfectly satisfied with life. Once a man contemplates Him, in the integrity of his heart, he knows his need.

Dayuma tells them what she knows. They sit as they do at any time in their houses, quite innocent of any idea of reverence. Dawa searches her ribs for chiggers, Mankamu picks her son

Dika's teeth, Uba inspects the foot fungus of her daughter and exhibits it to her neighbor. Gikita and Kumi watch the birds and comment on their flight. A row of little naked boys, clad in their Sunday-go-to-meeting skein of string, sits on a log in front of Dayuma. They are spellbound by the story of Jesus stilling the storm at sea. Some of the old women find it hard to concentrate. They have their own stories—stories of their own people, their husbands, their fathers, how they were killed, how they used to live. Why listen to this story of a man who lived so far away, so very long ago? He was a foreigner. What had this to do with them? And surely, even if He had something to say to them, it did not involve obedience. If Dayuma tells them that He said they must not kill, is this simply because it is not the foreigners' custom to kill?

The Auca, too, believes that it is wrong to kill—*except* under certain conditions. He has a conscience about killing. Some of the men who killed the five missionaries say now that they did not do well to kill them. But it was only a mistake. The Auca was trying to preserve his own way of life, his own liberty. He believed the foreigners were a threat to that liberty. He had every right—indeed, he did what he considered the noble thing—to kill them. In America we do not merely excuse a man for defending his country—we decorate him. And the more efficiently we kill, the more commendable our military tactics. Clearly, if man's inhumanity to man is the issue, American civilization has little to offer the Amazon Indian. Deathblows are dealt—no matter if it be with wooden spears or ballistic missiles.

The message we had come to communicate went straight to the heart of things. It could not deal with the peripheral. Yet the language which was to be our medium seemed to be limited to the peripheral. It is true that the Aucas had a word for God. They thought of Him as the one who had made men. The name was the same as for a species of fish. Dayuma knew of no pejorative connotation in this term so she used it in speaking of God. The word for son is the same as the word for child, of whatever age or sex. So in speaking of God's Son we used exactly the same words we would use in speaking of the offspring of the fish. What possibility was there that the Indians would grasp anything He said?

We know that it is not the words that give life. Even God chose to limit Himself to the use of human language. And we are led to hope that through mere words—no matter what the study and translation of those words may cost—the Spirit of God may show men the person of Jesus Christ, who is the Living Word. It is in the belief that He is the Son of God that the Aucas may have life. "The letter kills. The Spirit giveth life."

11

Neither Foreigner nor Savage

T HERE WERE SOME very long days in the jungle when the Aucas
all went off fishing or planting and left us entirely alone.
There were peaceful nights when they fell asleep early and I lay in
my hammock by the embers and read by candlelight. Sometimes
it was the Bible. Sometimes it was the transcription of an Auca
tape. Other times I read an American news magazine, dropped to
me from the airplane. Suddenly a night breeze or a moth put the
candle out and I was jerked from the pages of that world—the
world of art, books, business, education—back to this one, this
moonlit jungle clearing, the quiet people asleep with their feet
over the fires, the little girl who was a part of both worlds, rolled
in her blanket on a bamboo bed beside me.

"In a universe suddenly divested of illusions and lights, man
feels an alien, a stranger."[1] When the candle went out and pictures were no longer visible, when the shrill cacophony of the
jungle night rose again to my consciousness and I saw those feet

[1]Albert Camus, *The Myth of Sisyphus*, Vintage Books, New York, 1959.

in the fireglow, I wanted some reconciliation, some clarification. On what plane would these worlds be reconciled? I asked God for the answers, and tried to learn what He wanted to teach me through this insulation: insulation from my own world by distance, insulation from the Auca world by lack of communication.

They had been called savage. Their habitat was known in the travel ads as the "Green Hell." I was called a missionary. I must communicate.

The "Green Hell" proved to be a paradise at times, although I never appreciated the mold, mildew, or mud of the jungle. I did love the towering trees, the delicate fungi, the endless display of bromeliads and mosses, ferns and flowers, the clear-running streams, the jewel-colored sunbirds. I did not like living in a house with no walls, but I loved having no housework to do. I missed the stimulation of conversation in my own language, but I was fascinated by the mysteries of a new one. I longed to put on a dress and high heels once in a while, but I was grateful for the carefree ease of Quichua skirt and blouse and bare feet. I wished Valerie had some playmates who would not always submit to her will, but I did not overlook the invaluable experiences she was having—simplicity is the purest breeding. For everything that I would have called an inconvenience there was compensation if I took the time to look for it and had the grace to be grateful.

I watched the people I had called savages. Somehow immortal in their nakedness, speaking together in the subdued tones used among Indians, laughing childishly over small things, interested in the tiniest events about them, they seemed a lovely contrast to the elaborate dress, the loud voices (the Quichuas do not say that we "speak" English—we "shout" it), the sophisticated humor, the world-consciousness of our civilization. There were other times when their crudeness, their limited interests, their incomprehensible language, their everlasting meddling with my possessions and my affairs, their pitilessness, and their abject poverty of soul depressed me terribly.

What did it really mean to be a missionary? Never mind the definitions I had held for six previous years of missionary work. I had to start all over again, from scratch. If we call ourselves followers of Jesus, obviously we must walk the path He walked.

"The Son of Man came not to be ministered unto, but to minister." We must get this straight. We have come, not to be benefactors, but to be *servants*. "Slaves" is the word Jesus often used. Our perception of this truth will make an incalculable difference in our attitude toward the people, which in turn cannot help but affect their attitude toward us. To be a benefactor is to be a superior. Quite apart from the rightness or wrongness, morally, of this view, I became aware that it was a bad mistake. To the Auca I was not a superior by any standards. To be a servant is to be an inferior, and unless we are willing to accept this position we are not followers of Jesus Christ. The servant is not greater than his lord. And lest we think there is some merit in what we do, we are reminded that when we have done all we are still "unprofitable." We are in debt. We owe it to Christ, we owe it to men, savage or civilized, to lay down our lives daily.

I had understood this only very dimly when I went to live with the Aucas. I had worked before among Indians who had known the white man and his ways and had to some degree at least bowed to the white man's "superiority." The Auca had no such idea. He had not a reason in the world for thinking of us as his betters, and he probably had some very valid reasons of his own for thinking of us as inferiors. But from all appearances, he accepted us in the beginning as equals. This was what I had thought I had wanted. Something happened one day which illuminated to me the falsity of my own position.

I was sitting in my leaf house with a clay pot near at hand. Two old women were in the house a few yards away. "Gikari!" one of them called, in the urgent half-whisper which is their way of shouting. "Bring that pot here." It was my pot but I took it to her. "Well—don't bring it *empty*. Go get some water in it."

I had to go down to the river by means of a log which lay at a steep angle, fill the pot, and carry it (it had no handles and was very heavy) back up the slippery log. The old woman took it without a word.

I pondered what I had meant before when I had talked about a desire to be "accepted." I had meant that I wanted to enjoy all the benefits of being a member of their society without its obligations, as well as the benefits of being a foreigner without its opprobrium. After all, I realized now, why shouldn't Dyiku order me to bring her water? She was an older woman. In Auca society she had a right to order the younger.

This helped me to understand a little better the position of a missionary. My reason for being a missionary was one of the few things I had never doubted. I knew one thing—I must obey God, and I believed this was the thing He meant me to do, just as He meant others to be fishermen, tax collectors, draftsmen, housewives. The role seemed incidental. The goal was all-important.

There remained the message which I had to communicate. In a sense, all that we did while living with the Aucas was an attempt at communication. To eat what they ate, to live in the same kind of house, to swim and fish with them, to teach them to blow up a balloon or whistle on their fingers, to learn to spin cotton thread or weave a hammock as they did, to listen hour after hour after hour to their stories and try to write down what they said—all this was communication, the attempt to understand, to relate ourselves to them and to reach as far as possible across the chasm which separated us. Many times this seemed a naïve hope. Many times I despaired of ever really knowing them, the secrets of their hearts. Then I realized that I did not know my own heart. In this we were one.

The Aucas are men. Human beings, made in the image of God. Macdonald said, "No matter how His image may have been defaced in me, the thing defaced is His image—an image yet, that can hear His word." We have a common source, common needs, common hopes, a common end. Carl Sandburg observes that we are "alike in all countries and tribes in trying to read what sky, land, and sea say to us. . . . Alike in the need of love, food, clothing, work, speech, sleep, fun—needs so alike, so inexorably alike." The lucid recognition of the Auca as my kinsman was at the same time a new acknowledgment of Jesus Christ, of our common need of Him.

Epilogue

THIS BOOK WAS written after I had spent only one of the two years that I lived with the Aucas. I had been in missionary work (first with Colorado Indians, then with Quichuas, then with Aucas) for about eight years and a furlough was due. When I went back to New Jersey I was pleased to learn that my friends at Harper and Row wanted to publish a book of my Auca photographs. I was an amateur in picture-taking, as Cornell Capa's foreword explains. It was my impression that I would be asked only to write captions for the pictures, but I found that the publishers wanted at least fifty thousand words, so *The Savage My Kinsman* was the result—one woman's observations, during one brief year, of a remote and fascinating people. My second year with them was incomparably easier in at least three ways: we had an airstrip, so the journey in and out took fifteen minutes instead of three days from Arajuno; Valerie and I lived in a house with walls (built for us by visiting Quichuas and soon copied by some of the Aucas); and I could by that time speak the Auca language nearly as well as Valerie, who turned six that year.

The house with walls had become a physical necessity. If you are going to live exactly as Aucas live, you must do exactly what Aucas do—and *nothing else*. I had two jobs to do which represented a radical departure from Auca ways: write down their language so that we could give them the Bible, and teach Valerie her schoolwork by correspondence course. These were desk jobs, and if you have a desk, it is a good idea to have a floor under it and some semblance of walls around it, especially in an area where rainfall exceeds twelve feet per year. Even in this "civilized" house there were still a good many distractions for both of us. For Valerie it was a tough struggle to concentrate on school books when small friends were breathing down her neck, trying out the crayons, flipping through the picture books, or begging her to come for a swim. I began to feel that the better part of wisdom would be to go where she would have competition of the sort that is more conducive to study.

That was one part of my reason for thinking of leaving Tiwaenu, but, certain as I was that God had led me there, I could not leave without equally clear direction. It came by the end of our second year, but in a bewildering though nonetheless compelling way. The other part of the reason has been explained by others, and from various points of view, none quite the same as mine.

George Macdonald wrote, "I would not favor a fiction to keep a whole world out of hell. The hell that a lie would keep any man out of is doubtless the very best place for him to go. It is truth . . . that saves the world" (*Annals of a Quiet Neighborhood*, chapter 9).

It is the truth that I want to tell here, but it cannot be the whole truth, not because of any desire to gloss over facts which ought to be stated, much less to "favor a fiction." For one thing I don't know all of the truth, only my side of it. For another I must be brief. But people ask, and some explanation is due.

There were differences between Rachel Saint and me. My conviction grew that the clearing in Tiwaenu was too small to accommodate two missionaries who were not in any strictly truthful sense really working together. One of us, it appeared, must go. My decision was a painful one.

Two opposite trends in current Christian thinking are danger-ous. One is the sheer triumphalism which is the coin of much reli-gious telecasting. Make it appealing. Make it cheap. Make it easy. Be a Christian and watch your difficulties dissolve. Obey God and everything you touch will turn to gold. The other is the ex-posé. Out of a very muddy notion of something called equality, and perhaps also out of an exaggerated fear of hero-worship or cultism, springs an urge to spy out all weaknesses and inconsis-tencies and thereby discredit practically all human effort, es-pecially when its intention is an unselfish one.

We must recognize the treacherous Scylla and Charybdis of missionary reporting—not telling enough of the story, and telling altogether too much. The first temptation is to minimize what is great. The second is to magnify what is trivial.

We must also recognize that as long as we are in these (Paul calls them "vile") bodies, our attempts to offer salvation and life will be mixed with corruption and death. Because of the earnest-ness and obedience of five men the Auca Indians were finally reached. But the men died. The world noted their death with awe, with cynicism, with indifference. Some Christians were aroused to missionary responsibility. Nine children were left fatherless. The example their fathers set for them, however, re-mains a strong and noble one. Much that was true appeared in Christian publications regarding this story. So did much that was false. (I was reported to have lost my mind, become an alcoholic, produced an Auca baby. Rachel was "massacred" by one report-er, she told me in a recent letter.) Mission boards struggled over the questions of "territory," credits, priorities, promotion. Most disagreements were worked out. The Aucas heard the gospel. They also got polio. Some died from it, others were crippled. Oil companies (more than a score, I'm told) have been able to enter what were formerly forbidden areas, so that the Indians now have tools, short-wave radios, hypodermic syringes and penicil-lin, helicopter pads, and hard hats. It is hardly necessary to point out that for every civilized "blessing" there seem often to be ten curses. The hunting grounds on which the Indians depended for food are being systematically destroyed by the search for petroleum. Efforts by missionaries to secure protection for them by the government have proved inadequate. Sam, Dayuma's son, the object of a great deal of interest and prayer, was given a Christian education in Quito and the United States, but has returned to live part-time in the city, part-time in the jungle, where he runs a tourist business. His view of missions and missionaries is a jaundiced one, to say the least.

How we long to point to something—anything—and say, "*This* works! *This* is sure!" But if it is something other than God Himself we are destined for disappointment. There is only one ultimate guarantee. It is the love of Christ. *The love of Christ.* Nothing in heaven or earth or hell can separate us from that, and because God is God and loves us He will not allow us to rest anywhere but in that Love. We run straight to Him when other refuges fail. Our misconceptions are corrected in Him, our failures redeemed, our sins cleansed, our griefs turned to joy. But first "the life also of Jesus must be manifest in our mortal bodies." First the drama must be played out—through suffering, weakness, failure, death, and resurrection.

Jesus came not to make us comfortable by satisfying our whims and acceding to our wishes and our sometimes foolish hopes, but to cast fire on the earth, to bring a sword. The old prophet Simeon saw, when Jesus was only eight days old, that He was "destined to cause the falling and rising of many . . . and to be a sign that will be spoken against." To Mary he promised "a sword will pierce your own soul too" (Luke 2:34, 35, NIV).

It is always hard to keep a "single eye," to look at things spiritually, especially when they look a mess. There are times, I confess, when the whole Tiwaenu scene strikes me as high comedy, though I haven't forgotten the tears. Imagine us—two such different women, different from each other, positively freakish to the Aucas, with a small blonde girl—going into that hidden clearing in the forest, moving into one of those houses which didn't amount to much more than an umbrella, eating whatever handouts we could get (I drew the line at ants and grubs), having powdered milk, salt, oatmeal—even chocolate and cheese sometimes—dropped to us by parachute ("There's certainly no virtue in being hungry!" Rachel said one day), asking stupid questions

("Why the string?" "How come you have holes in your earlobes?" "Why do you shave your temples, pluck out all your eyebrows?" "Will this wood burn?" "Is that plant edible?"), putting ideas into their heads (the wearing of clothes, the use of matches, aluminum pots, scissors, soap), depending upon them for everything and thus becoming three nuisances, complaining about the smoke in our eyes, the gnats, the mud, the rain, lining people up to take pictures, shutting them up to listen to God's word, criticizing their morals, objecting to the rude noises they made during Dayuma's Sunday morning "sermons," and generally turning upside down their whole view of life and the world. Imagine!

God keep us from sitting in the seat of the scornful, concentrating solely on the mistakes, the paltriness of our efforts, the width of the gap between what we hoped for and what we got. How shall we call this "Christian" work? What are we to make of it?

We must not proceed from our own notions of God's action (it will appear He has not acted) but must look clearly and unflinchingly at what happens and seek to understand it through the revelation of God in Christ. His life on earth had a most inauspicious beginning. There was the scandal of the virgin birth, the humiliation of the stable, the announcement not to village officials but to uncouth shepherds. A baby was born—a Savior and King—but hundreds of babies were murdered because of Him. His public ministry, surely no tour of triumph, no thundering success story, led not to stardom but to crucifixion. Multitudes followed Him, but most of them wanted what they could get out of Him and in the end all His disciples fled. Yet out of this seeming weakness and failure, out of His very humbling to death, what exaltation and what glory. For the will of God is not a quantitative thing, static and measurable. The Sovereign God moves in mysterious relation to the freedom of man's will. We can demand no instant reversals. Things must be worked out according to a divine design and timetable. Sometimes the light rises excruciatingly slowly. The Kingdom of God is like leaven and seed, things which work silently, secretly, slowly, but there is in them an incalculable transforming power. Even in the plain soil, even in the dull dough, lies the possibility of transformation for, as the psalmist wrote, "All things serve Thee."

The missionary, with all his sin and worldliness, stands nevertheless with Christ for the salvation of the world. As I learned when I was with the "savages," they do not need Christ *more* than I do, for we are all of us sheep who have turned every one to his own way. If I know who the Shepherd is and how to find Him, it is surely my duty to do what I can to point other sheep to Him. The effort to do this must not be seen in "either/or" terms—either it is flawless, and therefore a success, or it is flawed, and therefore a miserable failure.

Every time my hopes are dashed I am asked to exchange my small view of "good" (when things work my way) for God's view of it, expressed in Romans 8: "God who searches our inmost being knows what the Spirit means, because he pleads for God's people in God's own way; and in everything, as we know, he cooperates for good with those who love God and are called according to his purpose. . . . that they should be shaped to the likeness of his Son." That, in the last analysis, is for us the only good—that shaping, no matter what it takes.

It cannot be accidental that I should find, this winter afternoon in a house on the stern coast of Massachusetts, Christina Rossetti's poem, underlined and dated from those last months in Tiwaenu. The date, I find to my astonishment, is precisely twenty years ago today. These are the lines:

I have no wit, no word, no tears;
My heart within me like a stone
Is numbed too much for hopes or fears;
Look right, look left, I dwell alone;
I lift mine eyes, but dimmed with grief
No everlasting hills I see;
My life is in the falling leaf;
O Jesus, quicken me.

My life is like a faded leaf,
My harvest dwindled to a husk;
Truly my life is void and brief
And tedious in the barren dusk;
My life is like a frozen thing,

No bud nor greenness can I see:
Yet rise it shall—the sap of Spring;
O Jesus, rise in me.

My life is like a broken bowl,
A broken bowl that cannot hold
One drop of water for my soul
Or cordial in the searching cold;
Cast in the fire the perished thing,
Melt and remould it, till it be
A royal cup for Him my King:
O Jesus, drink of me.

I had forgotten that I had had the little blue volume of Rossetti's verses with me in Tiwaenu (though the ravages of tropical humidity and the crickets that lived in my house are obvious). It was a gift from my brother Tom. I have picked it up from time to time over the years since, but am not really familiar with most of the pages. Reading the above lines today I remember something of the discouragement and isolation I must have felt when I marked them. I also know beyond the least doubt that the prayers have been and continue to be answered.

* * *

The little blonde girl in the pictures is now the wife of a minister, Walter D. Shepard Jr., of Laurel, Mississippi. They have a son named Walter III who will soon be four years old, and a daughter named after her grandmother Elisabeth. She will be two in a few months.

Rachel Saint remained with the Aucas until 1976. She lives now in Dallas where her mission board, Wycliffe Bible Translators, has a headquarters.

My husband Lars Gren and I live in Magnolia, Massachusetts.

According to the latest report, five missionaries are with the Aucas. The translation of the Bible into their language goes on.

Magnolia, Massachusetts
January 1, 1981

Books by Elisabeth Elliot

The Savage My Kinsman—photographs and text describing a year with the Auca Indians of Ecuador.

Love Has a Price Tag—a collection of essays on varied topics.

A Lamp for My Feet—Brief meditations which apply the Bible to the common experience of twentieth-century living.

Shadow of the Almighty—the life of Jim Elliot, including his personal journals and letters, his love story, his missionary experience.

These Strange Ashes—the story of a missionary's first year, touching on the questions of apparent failure and loss.

Through Gates of Splendor—the story of five missionaries killed in Ecuador by Auca Indians in 1956.

Let Me Be a Woman—Notes for Valerie on what it means to be a woman, single, married, or widowed.

The Journals of Jim Elliot

The Mark of a Man—notes for Pete on the responsibilities assigned to men by God; the meaning of masculinity.

Discipline: The Glad Surrender—what it means to accept the lordship of Christ in one's body, mind, emotions, time, work, etc.

Passion and Purity—a true love story, illustrating the principles by which to preserve "the gift you give only once," virginity.

No Graven Image—a novel probing the question of God's sovereignty.

A Slow and Certain Light—on the guidance of God and how a Christian may discover His will.

The Liberty of Obedience—on Christian maturity and service; on what a Christian is "allowed" to do.